ABLETON GROOVES

quick PRO
guides

ABLETON GROOVES

Programming Basic and Advanced Drum Grooves with Ableton Live

Josh Bess

Hal Leonard Books
An Imprint of Hal Leonard Corporation

Published in 2013 by Hal Leonard Books
An Imprint of Hal Leonard Corporation
7777 West Bluemound Road
Milwaukee, WI 53213

Trade Book Division Editorial Offices
33 Plymouth St., Montclair, NJ 07042

Printed in the United States of America

Book design by Adam Fulrath
Book composition by Kristina Rolander

Library of Congress Cataloging-in-Publication Data is available upon request.

ISBN 9781480345744

www.halleonardbooks.com

CONTENTS

Contents

Chapter 3

Chapter 4

Chapter 5

ACKNOWLEDGMENTS

This project has been supported by an amazing group of individuals, who all creatively nurtured my original idea, giving life to it in the form of *Ableton Grooves*.

To Tanya Lam, Paul Lemarquis, Erico Wakamatsu, Stephanie Fung, Victor Rhee, Henry Kim, Adriano Clemente, Greg Gibaldi, Andrew Kokkosis, Catherine Scalia, Megan Faye, Robert Mitrea, Drew "Drumz" Bertrand, Chris "Tomato" Harfenist…I say thank you. Because of you, this book is all I hoped it would be. Thank you so much for your support and contribution to this project.

Bill Gibson and the Hal Leonard team deserve a special thanks as well. Your support and enthusiasm for this project helped give it the home it needed. I could not thank you enough for being a part of this project.

Lastly, this would not have been possible without my family. My incredible parents, Sid and Susan, have supported and contributed to my passions, ideas and goals from the beginning. Thank you so much for being the inspiring parents you are! My siblings, Adam, Jen, Elana, and Alexa, your strong support helped motivate me to complete this project from when it was just a spark of an idea. Thank you all so much for your continued love and support!

And, to the endless list of family and friends, you know who you are…so thank you all!

ABLETON GROOVES

INTRODUCTION

Welcome to *Ableton Grooves*, the groove encyclopedia for mapping out MIDI to create realistic-sounding drums for various styles of music. In this book you'll learn not only how to read the exercises given, but also how to use them as tools to develop your own musical ideas. We also cover getting started with Ableton Live, reading notated music, reading MIDI mappings, techniques to transform your programmed drums to sound as real as possible, and more than 80 standard drum set grooves of many styles!

What Is Ableton Grooves All About?

Ableton Grooves is a book designed to help anybody and everybody learn to program all styles of drum kit grooves with the use of MIDI programming. It will help musicians from the most basic levels all the way to advanced players and programmers. *Ableton Grooves* teaches you more than mapping out beats and grooves; it will hopefully become a stepping-stone to a new way of thinking and creating. The main purpose behind *Ableton Grooves* is to introduce new styles of music and grooves that you have possibly never played, programmed, or even heard of before, along with tips and tricks to create something new for yourself.

What Is MIDI?

In 1983, the first Musical Instrument Digital Interface (MIDI) was created, which changed the world of digital music. MIDI is known as a universal digital language used by computers to communicate and share information about musical notes, pitch, attack velocities, release times, and more. This language, a binary code that all computers understand, uses zeros and ones to communicate data between computers, keyboards, controllers, and so on.

To this day, MIDI is a music industry standard for digital communication that lets MIDI Instruments, MIDI controllers, and computer software talk to each other in order to play back and record music. More and more of the music you hear today is written, recorded, and even played live with MIDI.

Because you're reading this book, I assume that you're a drummer or a programmer who wants to program realistic-sounding drums. If that is the case, then you will love this next piece of information, and if not, read it anyway because it's very exciting. Before the development of MIDI, musicians had to lug around loads of gear to create the sounds they wanted for a live show or studio recording. Today, for a live performance or studio setting you could compact all of the instruments you desire into a MIDI-compatible sound library along with a MIDI keyboard, MIDI drum kit, or even a MIDI sampler touch pad and perform with the sounds of a drum kit, congas, bongos, timbales, shakers, cowbells, djembes, taiko drums, gongs, bells, timpani, and more all at your fingertips! And with detailed samples and sound design, they'll sound like the real thing!

I don't want you to be confused, thinking that MIDI Notes are the actual sounds you are hearing as, for example a kick drum, a snare hit, or even piano notes. I'll say it now, to make it perfectly clear: MIDI does not transmit an audio signal! That being said, MIDI transmits data, which is then recognized by a sound module to trigger a sound in the modules library.

Still confused? Here's an example: All MIDI-compatible controllers and MIDI-compatible software follow the same MIDI language, meaning they all interpret any given MIDI message the same way. If you play a middle C on a MIDI keyboard, that key is not being recognized as middle C. It is being recognized as a MIDI Note. We'll choose the number 1 for now, and refer to that key as MIDI Note #1. We then want that key to play the sound of a snare drum. We will use a sound module with a snare drum sample in its sound library, Ableton Live's Drum Rack for example, then map out MIDI Note #1 to trigger the sound of the Snare Drum. Whether MIDI Note #1 is being played off of a MIDI keyboard or a MIDI touch pad, or mapped out by hand in any computer software, MIDI Note #1 will send the same information to your sound module to produce your snare drum sound.

What If I Don't Play Drums or Read Music?

Ableton Grooves, being an instructional guide for programming drums using MIDI, teaches in a way that you don't need to know how to play an actual drum kit or know how to read notated music. The MIDI Map on each page will show you exactly where to place your MIDI Notes with the placement of the beat, duration, and the velocity value. Then why have notated music in the book, you ask? Being able to read notated music is a great tool for understanding the musical language, for both the player and the programmer. For those who know how to read music, comparing the notated rhythms with the MIDI mapped rhythms could help with the understanding of where the beats are placed, before even hearing the groove. Throughout this book, I provide both notated music and MIDI Maps for every groove.

So once again, don't worry if you cannot read notated music. You'll still be able to use this book! From hearing each audio sample of the groove, seeing the MIDI Maps, and referring to the notated music on every page, it will come naturally to understand this musical language even if it's foreign to you at the moment. Use your eyes and ears to distinguish what you are seeing on the page and what you are hearing from the audio samples—it will be easier than you think.

Chapter 1

GETTING STARTED

Ready to get started? In this chapter, I will introduce you to Ableton Live 9, along with jumping into drum programming right away. If you're not familiar with Ableton Live 9, don't worry. We'll quickly and efficiently go through the basics along with sharing great tips and tricks that will help with your understanding of Ableton Live 9 and drum programming. This chapter works all the way from basic installation of Ableton Live 9 to programming and mixing your own first drum groove.

Ableton Suite 9 Demo Installation

If you do not already own Ableton Live, install the 30-day free trial of Ableton Suite 9 that's on the DVD-ROM that accompanies this book.

To install, open the Ableton Live 9 Demo folder, on the DVD-ROM. Depending on your operating system, open the folder, Mac or PC, and work through the following instructions. You will have the choice to install the 32-bit or 64-bit version of Ableton Live Suite 9.

Figure 1-1. Mac

Figure 1-2. PC

- For any Ableton Live updates, please refer to: www.ableton.com/en/trial/.

Josh Bess Acoustic Kits Installation

To install your Drum Kits into Ableton Live, you will first need to have Ableton Live installed on your computer.

- Within the included Ableton Grooves DVD, double-click to open up the file named Josh Bess Acoustic Kits.alp.
- You will then be asked to install the package; click "Install."
- You can find these kits within your Live 9 Browser, under the following folder: Packs/Josh Bess Acoustic Kits/Drums.

Intro to Ableton Live

All right, now that you have Ableton Live and your Drum Kits installed, let's upload a kit and get started! If you have never used Ableton Live before, don't worry; it's easy to get started with the following basic steps.

Open the Live 9 Browser

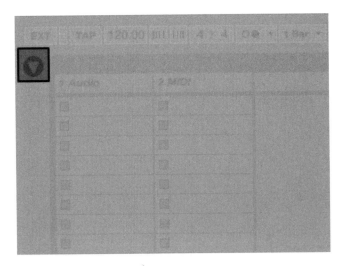

Figure 1-3

- The first thing we're going to do is open the Live 9 Browser.
- Click on the arrow symbol facing down, on the left hand side of your screen. When the browser is open, it will appear like this:

Figure 1-4

Open Packs Folder

- Next, open the Packs Section within the Live 9 Browser by clicking on "Packs."

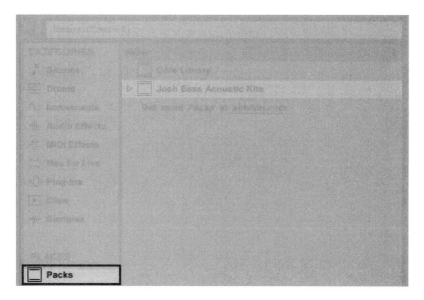

Figure 1-5

- Follow by opening the Josh Bess Acoustic Kits Pack by clicking on the arrow toggle switch.

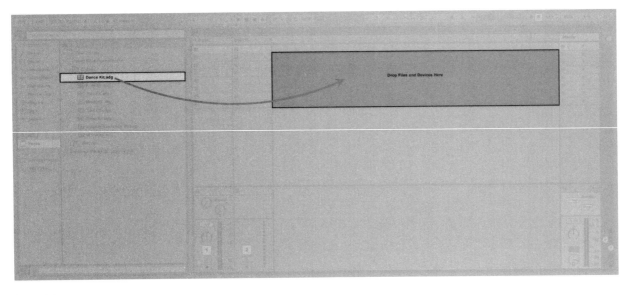

Figure 1-6

- Open the Drums folder and you will see the Drum Racks you will be programming with throughout this book.

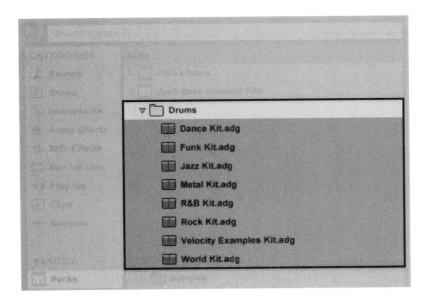

Figure 1-7

(Packs > Josh Bess Acoustic Kits > Drums)

Choose Your Drum Kit

For this example, let's try the Dance Kit. All you have to do is click and drag the Dance Kit into your session view, where it says Drop Files and Devices Here, in the center of your screen. This will automatically open up to a new MIDI Track titled Dance Kit.

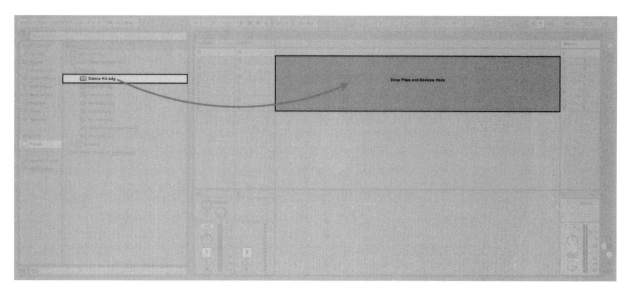

Figure 1-8

Tracks 1 (Audio) and 2 (MIDI) are not needed, so feel free to delete them by clicking on the track title bar, which will then become highlighted, and pressing the Delete key.

Figure 1-9

Create MIDI Clip

- A MIDI clip holds the MIDI data that you will soon be programming. On your new MIDI Track, you'll see a list of gray rectangles lined up vertically. These are called clip slots, which will soon hold your MIDI clip.

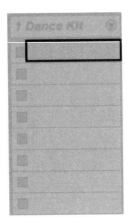

Figure 1-10

- To create a MIDI clip in your clip slot, double-click on a clip slot. Now your MIDI clip is created.

Figure 1-11

When you create a MIDI clip in an empty clip slot, you can see that the MIDI Note Editor automatically appears at the bottom of the screen. Let's take a closer look at the MIDI Note Editor.

MIDI Note Editor

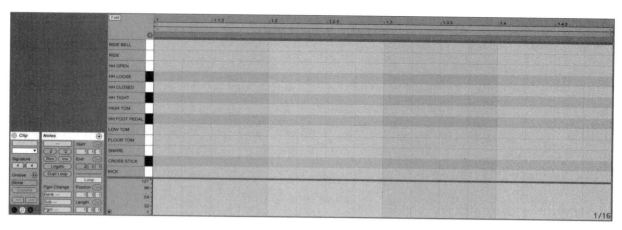

Figure 1-12

The MIDI Note Editor in Ableton Live is where we are going to write in our MIDI data, using a gridded map for easy writing and editing.

The first thing we're going to do is resize the Editor for a better visual. Make your Editor look similar to Figure 1-12.

- Do this by clicking on the light gray line above the Editor, and drag vertically to increase or decrease the size of the MIDI Note Editor.

Figure 1-13

Now, we're going to adjust the lower half of the MIDI Note Editor, which is the Velocity Editor.

- Do this by clicking and dragging the dark gray line above the Velocity Editor vertically to increase or decrease the size of the Velocity Editor. This dark gray line is the Velocity Editor View Split.

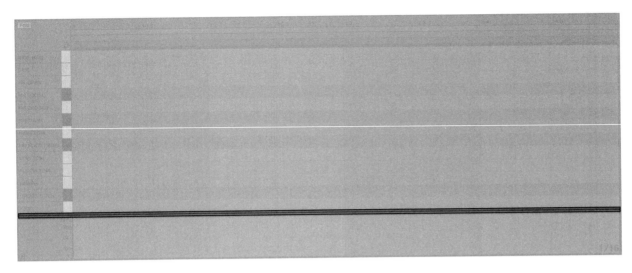

Figure 1-14

Okay! Now that your Editor is at a comfortable visual setting, let's move on!

Writing MIDI Notes

Let's get started writing some MIDI Notes into the MIDI Note Editor. MIDI Notes are going to be the data that tell your MIDI drum kit which sounds to play.

Now, let's create our first drum hit. We'll start off by creating a closed hi-hat sound.

- On the Editor, double-click on the first grid box to the right of the Piano Roll instrument, HH CLOSED

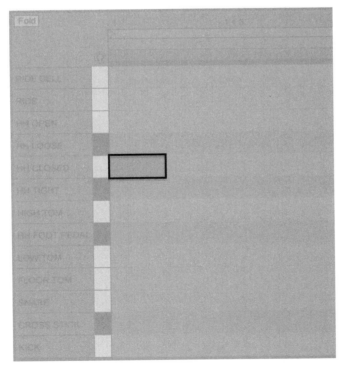

Figure 1-15

You've just created your first MIDI Note!

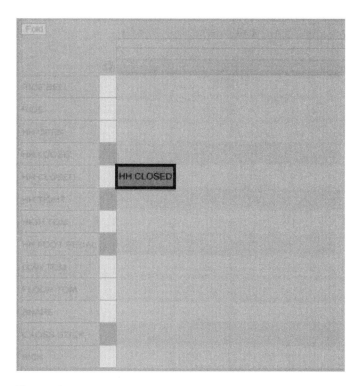

Figure 1-16

- Now, look at the Velocity Editor in Figure 1-17. Click-and-drag vertically on the velocity marker, bringing the marker to its full level (127).

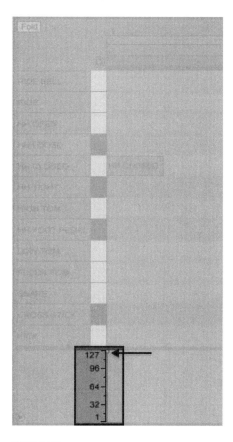

Figure 1-17

Let's hear what you've just created.

- For playback, click the Clip Launch button on the MIDI clip.

Figure 1-18

The great thing about Ableton Live is that you can still create, while listening to your playback in real time. While your clip is playing back, try creating more closed hi-hat notes on your Editor.

Try this out:

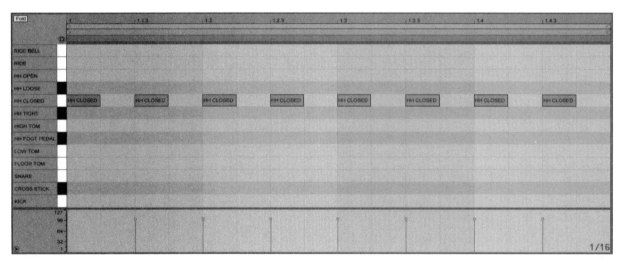

Figure 1-19

Great! Now what we want to do is highlight a group of these notes.

- Click-and-drag on the Editor, surrounding multiple notes with a rectangle, to highlight multiple notes.

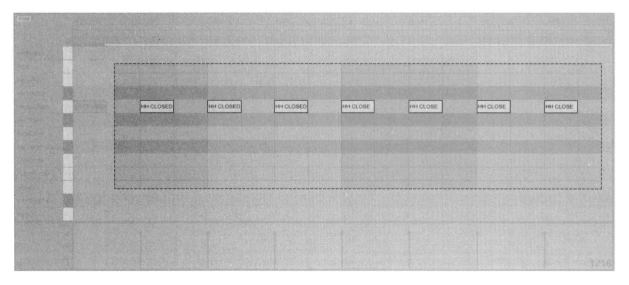

Figure 1-20

- Once these notes are highlighted, drag a velocity marker of any one of the highlighted notes, and they will all move together. Bring these notes up to a velocity of 127.

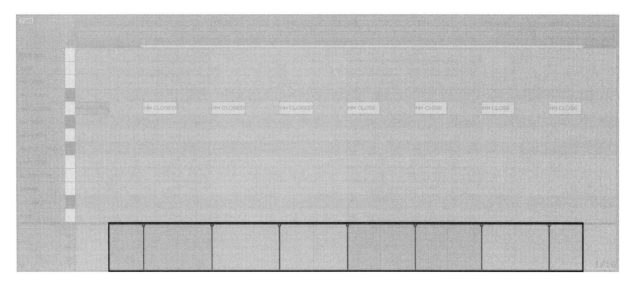

Figure 1-21

- You can add as many notes as you'd like on the Editor, having multiple sounds play at the same time. Try adding the sound of a snare drum to the groove. For the sound of a snare drum, write a MIDI Note on a grid box horizontal to the Piano Roll instrument Snare.

  Try this out: add a snare drum on beat 1.2 and beat 1.4 of the grid.

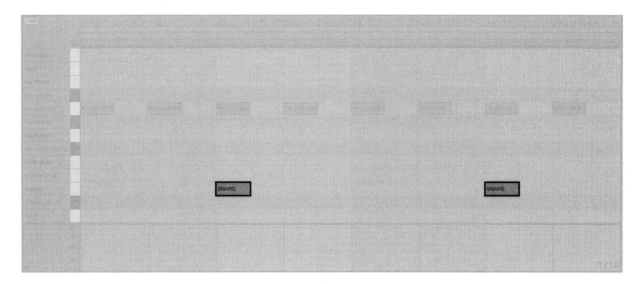

Figure 1-22

Try bringing both of those snare drums to 127 velocity as well!

Great! Now, let's add a kick drum to this groove.

For the sound of a kick drum, write a MIDI Note on a grid box horizontal to the Piano Roll instrument Kick.

Try this out: Add a kick drum on beat 1 and beat 1.3 of the grid.

Figure 1-23

Tip: Try drawing in notes using the Draw Mode. Click on the Draw Mode switch to enable Draw Mode, or use the hot key (B)

Figure 1-24

While in Draw Mode, simply click on the MIDI Note Editor to create or delete a MIDI Note. Click-and-drag across the MIDI Note Editor to draw multiple notes.

Congratulations, you've created your first drum groove! You can edit your MIDI Notes in real time playback as well. Try clicking and dragging the fourth HH Closed MIDI Note up to the HH Loose position.

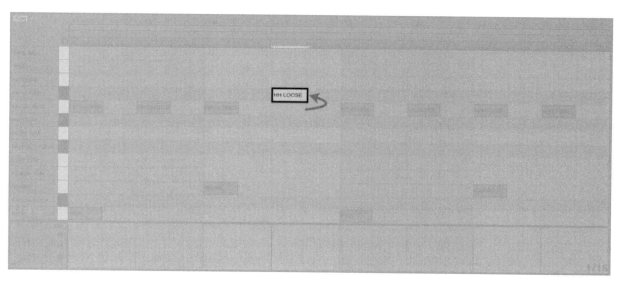

Figure 1-25

Wasn't that easy? Now you understand how to create and arrange your own drum kit grooves.

NOTE: Double-click on a MIDI Note to delete a single note. To delete multiple notes, drag over multiple notes to select them, then press the Delete key on your keyboard.

To stop playback, hit the space bar.

MIDI Note Editor

Now that you are familiar with writing MIDI Notes into your Editor, let's go through the basic parameters of the MIDI Note Editor. It might seem like a lot to remember, so feel free to return to this page to familiarize yourself with the Editor whenever needed. As you might have seen already, I will be giving you tips and notes throughout the book as well, for various ways to use these parameters.

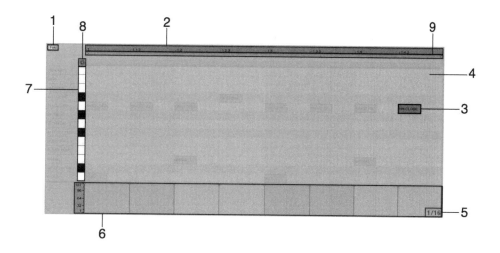

Figure 1-26

1. **Fold Button:** Activating this button will immediately hide all rows, or empty keys tracks, that are not associated with your Drum Rack. When activated, the titles of each drum pad are available along the left side of the Editor.

2. **Beat Time Ruler:** The beat time ruler is very important as it helps divide the grid into various bars and beats.

Example:

    1 = Beat 1
    1.2 = Beat 2
    1.3 = Beat 3
    1.4 = Beat 4

When scrolling the mouse above the beat time ruler, a magnifying glass icon appears. By clicking and dragging horizontally, you can scroll across the Editor. Clicking and dragging vertically zooms in and out of the Editor.

3. **Note:** Notes are your MIDI data that you are writing in to your MIDI Note Editor. You can either double-click on the Note Editor to write in a note, or you can click-and-drag in Draw Mode to write multiple notes consecutively. To enable Draw Mode, click on the pencil tool in the Control Bar or press the hot key [B]. When you click on a note, it darkens and is now in Edit Mode. The note can now be moved with the arrow keys or by clicking and dragging them to new positions. You can create and delete notes by double-clicking on them, and you can change the length by dragging the note edges.

Tip: When editing a note, here's a little trick to edit your note velocity. If you hold (command) on a Mac, or (ctrl) on a PC, before clicking on the note, drag vertically to increase or decrease the velocity amount of the highlighted MIDI Note.

4. **MIDI Note Editor:** This is the main Editor where you can write in your MIDI data. By double-clicking on the Note Editor, you write in your MIDI Notes. You can click-and-drag to select notes for editing on the Note Editor or enable the control bar's Draw Mode switch to draw notes.

5. **Marker Snap:** The Marker Snap is the number in the bottom right corner of the Editor. This number shows the current spacing between grid lines. To change this number, right-click anywhere on the grid of your MIDI Note Editor and choose one of the following grid settings under Fixed Grid, or press (command+1)/(command+2) on a Mac or (Ctrl+1)/(Ctrl+2) on a PC, to increase or decrease the grid value.

NOTE: The reason this is called the Marker Snap is, when moving your MIDI Notes on the grid, they will automatically be "snapped" to the grid line at the value of the Marker Snap.

Example:

    Quarter-note grid: 1/4
    Eighth-note grid: 1/8
    Sixteenth-note grid: 1/16
    Thirty-second-note grid: 1/32

6. **Velocity Editor:** Clicking and dragging vertically on the velocity markers can change MIDI Note velocities. Each velocity marker corresponds to the MIDI Note above—you can see this by clicking on the velocity marker—and it will highlight the corresponding note. You can click various velocity markers while holding the shift key to select multiple markers to edit. You can also enable the control bar's Draw Mode to draw markers.

NOTE: If there are no MIDI Notes in your Editor, you will not see any velocity markers. You can also expand the Velocity Editor by clicking and dragging vertically on the Velocity Editor View Split, which is just above the Velocity Editor.

7. **Piano Roll:** The Piano Roll is an important asset to the MIDI Note Editor, which helps locate, and corresponds to, specific notes on the grid. For example, if you write a MIDI Note on the grid, which is in the horizontal path as a Piano Roll note, you will be writing MIDI data to correspond with that specific Piano Roll note.

8. **MIDI Editor Preview:** Activate this button to listen to all changes or modifications made to MIDI Notes as they are created and moved. With MIDI Editor previewing, you can also click individual notes on the Piano Roll to listen to each sample.

9. **Loop Brace:** The Loop Brace defines the length of the clip's loop, when the Loop switch is enabled in the Notes Box. For example: Ableton Live MIDI clips are one bar long when first created. Most of the grooves you will be programming throughout this book are two bars long. To adjust the clip length, you will use the Notes Box to the left of your MIDI Note Editor.

- Click on the Show/Hide Notes Box to open the Notes Box.

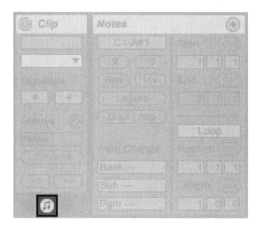

Figure 1-27

- Then, make sure the Loop switch is enabled.

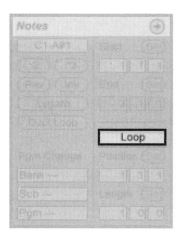

Figure 1-28

You can then adjust the length of your clip by clicking and dragging vertically or by typing in values to change the length of the Loop Brace.

- Simply, change the length from 1-0-0 to 2-0-0.

Figure 1-29

Tip: You could also drag the ends of the Loop Brace to widen or shorten the loop.

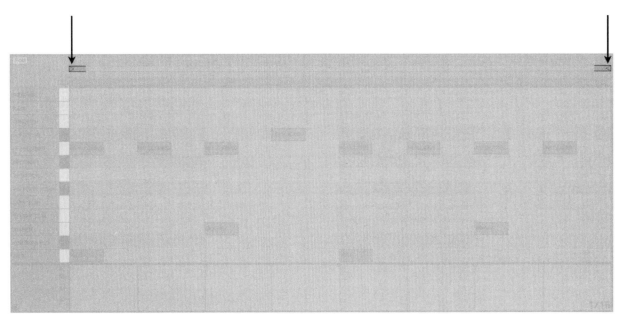

Figure 1-30

Now that you are familiar with the MIDI Note Editor, let me introduce the MIDI Map, which will be our way of reading the MIDI data we will be programming.

MIDI Map

The MIDI Map is what you will be reading from to program your MIDI data into your MIDI Note Editor. (Refer to Figure 1-26 for the MIDI Note Editor.) The layout is very simple, and is similar to the MIDI Note Editor except for two things.

- The velocity amount is written on the MIDI Notes, where on the MIDI Note Editor's MIDI Notes, it would say the instrument name. The reason for this is to give you an exact velocity number to guide your programming, without you having to guess the velocity amount by looking at the velocity markers.
- The grid value, similar to the MIDI Note Editor's Marker Snap, is now in the top left corner for a clear and easy visual.

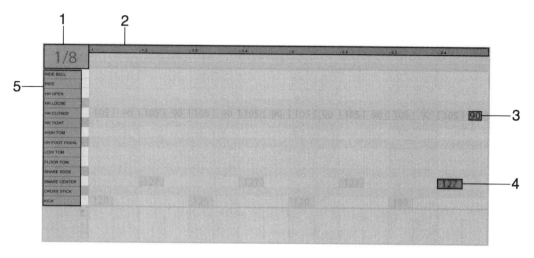

Figure 1-31

1. **Grid Value:** Specifies the current spacing between grid lines.

Example:

    1/4—Quarter-Note Grid

    1/8—Eighth-Note Grid

    1/8T—Eighth-Note Triplet Grid

    1/16—Sixteenth-Note Grid

    1/16T—Sixteenth-Note Triplet Grid

2. **Beat Time Ruler:** Divides the grid into bars and beats, corresponding to the grid value.

Example:

    1 = Beat 1 of measure 1

    1.2 = Beat 2 of measure 1

    1.3 = Beat 3 of measure 1

    1.4 = Beat 4 of measure 1

    2 = Beat 1 of measure 2

    2.2 = Beat 2 of measure 2

    2.3 = Beat 3 of measure 2

    2.4 = Beat 4 of measure 2

3. **Velocity:** The note's velocity will be written in the center of the MIDI Note. This number corresponds to the given note's velocity amount. In the Ableton Grooves Kits included, the velocity will correspond to the drum's dynamics. Low velocity is to soft dynamics, where high velocity is to loud dynamics.

4. **MIDI Note:** This represents where a MIDI Note will be placed on the MIDI Note Editor. Each note has a number written inside, This is the velocity amount of the note.

5. **Instrument:** The instrument text refers to the specific instrument within the Ableton Live Drum Rack. All instruments correspond to MIDI Notes written in the same horizontal grid path as the instrument text.

We are now ready to start programming!

Chapter 2
REAL FEEL

Here is where your programmed drums will really come to life. From the following examples, you will learn how to control the most precise drum hits with dynamics, precision, and groove, to create a realistic-feeling drum kit under your fingertips, literally!

Velocity Changes for Dynamics

All right now, just because you're working with electronic instruments doesn't mean you can't make them sound or feel like somebody is actually playing the part with a human, relaxed feel. Nobody wants to go to a concert and hear a drummer playing without dynamics, so why would you want your programmed drums to lack dynamics? With the use of accents and dynamics, you can easily make your programmed drums sound and feel like a real kit.

For Velocity Examples 1-5, we will be using the Velocity Examples Kit in your Ableton Live 9 Browser. (Packs > Josh Bess Acoustic Kits > Drums > Real Feel Examples Kit)

For these examples, we'll be focusing on a hi-hat sample, but this does not mean this can only be done with a hi-hat; it could be done with any and every sound sample included with this book. After completing the following exercises, have fun and explore what you could do with velocity and dynamics with all of your sound samples!

Velocity Example 1

Here is your first programming example with the use of the MIDI Map, which is based on a straight sixteenth-note hi-hat pattern played straight with no accents or dynamic changes.

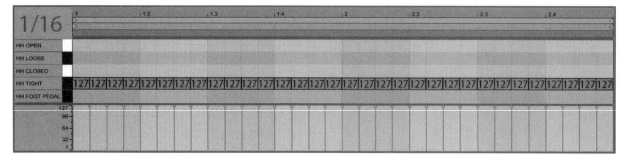

Figure 2-1

Hear how robotic this sounds? No feel, no dynamics.

> **NOTE:** Click on a MIDI Note to highlight, and press (Command + D) on a Mac, or (Control + D) on a PC, to duplicate the note, for quick and easy writing. To hear what you programmed, click the Clip Launch on the MIDI clip.

Once the clip is launched, pressing the space bar will stop and start playback.

Velocity Example 2

Here's the same sixteenth-note pattern, but with accents on every quarter beat.

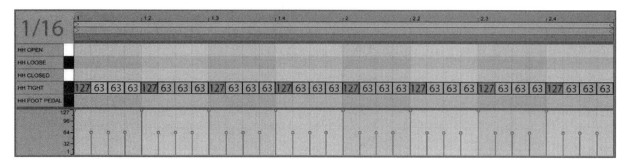

Figure 2-2

Hear how the slightest change of dynamics could change the feel of the pattern?

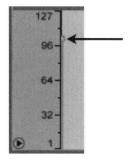

Figure 2-3

NOTE: Click-and-drag the velocity marker vertically to control velocity value. Move up to increase the velocity, and down to decrease the velocity. When changing the velocity, a number appears above your MIDI Note, to show the current velocity value.

Figure 2-4

Velocity Example 3

Here's the same sixteenth-note pattern with various accents.

NOTE: An accent is a hit of greater velocity, which is used to emphasize a particular note within a groove.

Notice how each hit is slightly different from the next, to create a sense of realistic touch to the sound.

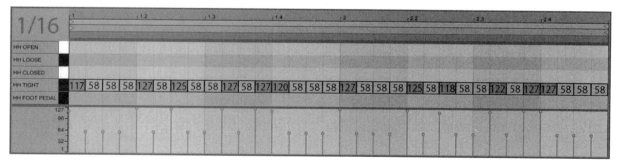

Figure 2-5

Now you really start hearing a groove happening, and it's only the hi-hat!

Velocity Example 4

Here is where you could really have fun. With the velocity changes, you could create hill-like figures going from soft to loud gradually, creating crescendos and decrescendos.

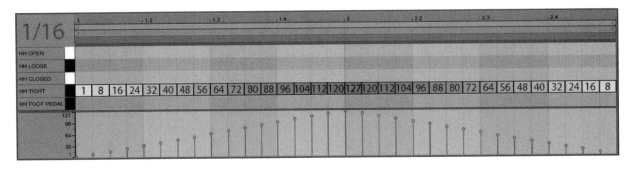

Figure 2-6

Tip: You can write with Draw Mode, enabling with the hotkey (B), in your Velocity Editor as well, for quick and easy writing. While in Draw Mode, just click and move your cursor to draw on the Velocity Editor. To exit Draw Mode, press (B) again.

Velocity Example 5

Here's the same sixteenth-note pattern with the use of all of the previous examples of accents, crescendos, and decrescendos.

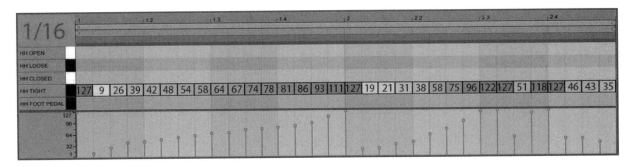

Figure 2-7

Hear the difference from Example 1? With various velocity changes, you could transform a robotic-programmed hi-hat pattern into a naturally felt musical groove.

Hi-Hat Programming

The hi-hats on a drum kit are two cymbals stacked on top of each other that can be opened and closed by a foot pedal, or hit with a drumstick. Combining the sounds of opening and closing the hi-hats along with hitting them with drumsticks could add great effect to a groove (and an endless amount of sounds). The hi-hat is a very noticeable and common sound for the drum kit in almost every style of music. There are so many ways to play and program a hi-hat, along with enhancing the drum's groove and style, based on the amount of precision and dynamics within each hit. Three common sounds from the hi-hat are the closed, loose, and open hits with a drumstick, meaning a drumstick is striking a tightly closed hi-hat, a loosely open hi-hat, and a completely open hi-hat. Another sound comes from closing the hi-hat with the foot pedal. There are many sounds that could be created by combining different velocities and variations of these sounds.

Take a listen to the Hi-Hat Examples audio samples, within the included DVD-ROM under the folder (Audio Samples/Real Feel Examples/Hi-Hat Examples). You will hear the tightly closed hi-hat, closed hi-hat, loose hi-hat, open hi-hat, and foot-closed hi-hat.

Hear the different options of sounds you could get from just one hi-hat?

Hi-Hat Example 1

For this example, we will use the closed hi-hat, and tight hi-hat, to create a rocking motion that is often used in Rock music for heavier accents of the quarter note. This replicates the sound of hitting the side of the hi-hat with the shoulder of a drumstick, while alternating the sound of hitting the top of the hi-hat with the tip of a drumstick.

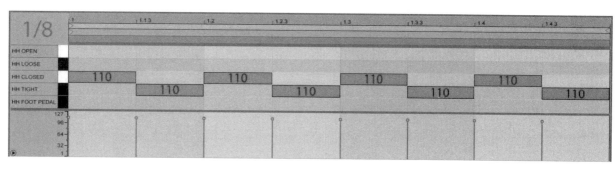

Figure 2-8

Hear how the closed hi-hat can add that accent to the beat? Try adding it on other beats, such as the upbeats of the groove, to create syncopated rhythms!

NOTE: Notice, this groove is only one bar long. Refer to the Notes Box on the left of the MIDI Note Editor and simply change the length value from 2-0-0 to 1-0-0.

Figure 2-9

Hi-Hat Example 2

Here is an example of the shortly opened hi-hat with a closed foot hi-hat on every downbeat. This will replicate the sound of only playing the hi-hat with the stick on the upbeats, while closing the hi-hat with a foot on the quarter-note downbeats.

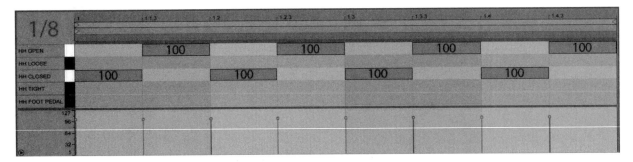

Figure 2-10

Hi-Hat Example 3

Here is a classic sound of the hi-hat being open for a specific beat in a groove. To do this, we will need to use the closed hi-hat and open hi-hat sound to create the effect that a drummer is opening the hi-hat with his or her foot for a specific beat, while continuing to hit the hi-hats with a drumstick. To do this we will need to add the sound of a closed hi-hat on the beat following the open hi-hat.

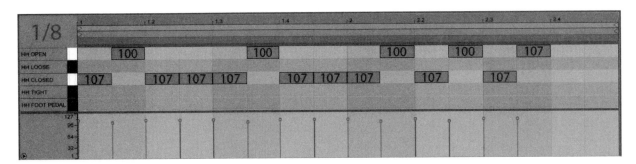

Figure 2-11

Hear how the open hi-hat doesn't ring out like it did in the Audio CD Sample Hi-Hat Open? By adding the closed hi-hat sound, you "choke" the sound of the open hi-hat. This choking effect comes into play with all of the hi-hat sounds.

NOTE: Notice, this groove is two bars long. Refer to the Notes Box on the left of the MIDI Note Editor and simply change the length value from 1-0-0 back to 2-0-0.

Figure 2-12

Hi-Hat Example 4

Here is an example using the closed hi-hat, and open hi-hat.

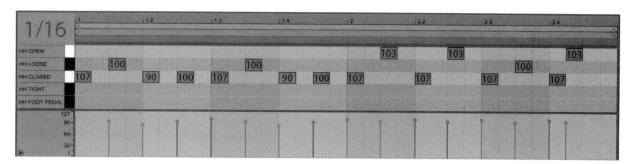

Figure 2-13

Hear the difference between the loose hi-hat and open hi-hat? They could create great effects within a groove, especially when you start messing around with the velocities as well.

Let's try this out on a full drum kit! For this example, open up the Dance Kit. (Packs > Josh Bess Acoustic Kits > Drums > Dance Kit)

Hi-Hat Example 5

Here is an example of the shortly opened hi-hat being used in a dance groove, with additional accents on the closed hi-hat. Open up the Dance Kit and program the groove in Figure 2-14.

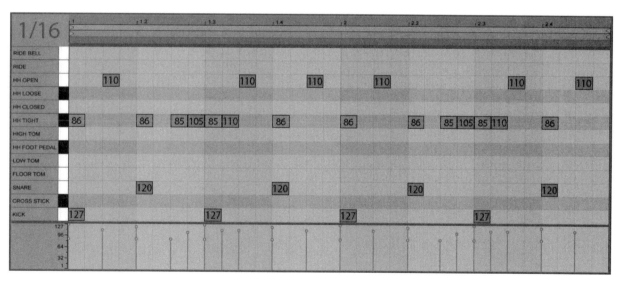

Figure 2-14

Hear all of the sounds that a hi-hat can produce? Throughout this book, there will be many grooves using the examples displayed previously in this chapter, so feel free to come back to this chapter to familiarize yourself with them. And once again, experiment with these sounds to create your own!

Mixing

Mixing is the process that allows you to create a more pleasing and aesthetic sound to your own music, whether that sound is cleaner, dirtier, smaller, wider, softer, or louder, the results are completely up to you to manipulate. Audio mixing is a full study of its own, but we will cover some of the basics, to get you started with mixing your drum kits in Ableton Live.

Mixing is a very important piece to your drum programming, for the reason that there are multiple instruments within a drum kit. For example, you have the kick drum, snare drum, toms, cymbals, and more, which depending how they are mixed, could completely change the sound, texture, and feel of your drum groove.

Let's get started with taking a look at the individual drums within your drum kit, along with the specific parameters that can be controlled.

Drum Rack Macro Controls

You have the freedom to control the pitch and reverb of each drum. To do this, click on the track title bar of your drum kit track.

Figure 2-15

On the bottom of the screen, your Dance Kit Device will appear and you can control the pitch knobs, which control the tone of each drum. Click-and-drag the Macro Controls vertically to increase or decrease the pitch of your kick drum, snare drum, or toms.

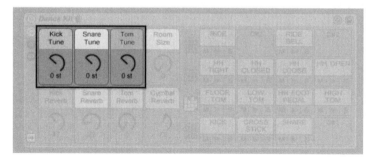

Figure 2-16

The reverb knobs control the amount of echo and decay of each drum, creating various spatial environments for each drum. Click-and-drag the Macro Controls vertically to increase or decrease the reverb amount.

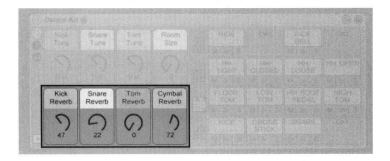

Figure 2-17

NOTE: The Room Size Macro controls the reverb of the entire drum kit, creating the effect of a larger or smaller room.

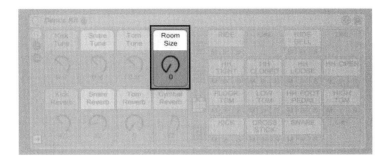

Figure 2-18

Chain Mixer

We also have the capability to adjust the volume of each individual drum.

- Simply click on the Chain Mixer fold button.

Figure 2-19

This will unfold the various drums within the Drum Rack, opening up a full mixer in Ableton Live's Session View.

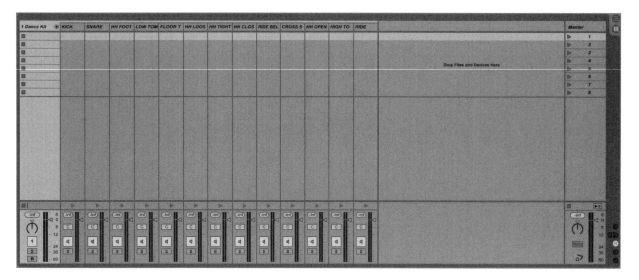

Figure 2-20

You will see each track has its own title in the track title bar, referring to each individual drum. In Figure 2-21, each track has its own volume slider, which controls the amount of volume output for each drum.

Figure 2-21

Click-and-drag vertically on the track volume slider to adjust the volume of each individual drum hit. You have the option to activate or solo each track by clicking on the Chain Activator or Chain Solo button. The Chain Activator will activate the chain, or deactivate it to mute this chain.

Figure 2-22

The Chain Solo will solo this chain, muting all others.

Figure 2-23

Panning

You can also adjust the panning of each drum, which is adjusting the stereo image of the chain. Simply click on the Chain Pan and drag vertically to adjust. This is simply moving the sound of the drum to the left, center, or right side of your stereo output.

Figure 2-24

By clicking and dragging on the right edge of the chain title bar horizontally, you can widen the chain and change the look of your mixer.

Figure 2-25

NOTE: The Chain Pan looks a little different now that it is larger, but it works in the same way. Try it out!

Figure 2-26

I've already adjusted the panning within the Drum Rack's samples, so you don't have to touch the panning too much, but feel free to make any changes you'd like!

Global Tempo

You can also adjust the speed of the groove, using Ableton Live's Global Tempo. The tempo is the speed of the groove, measured in BPM (beats per minute). If the tempo is set at 120, this means there are 120 beats every minute. You can adjust the tempo to your liking, whether that is faster or slower. In the top left corner of the screen, you will see your Global Tempo.

Figure 2-27

This is your current Global Tempo. Simply click-and-drag vertically to increase and decrease the tempo.

- Launch a clip with a drum groove programmed and try bringing the BPM down to 80.00. Hear the difference?

NOTE: Every groove in this book will have a tempo included, matching the Audio Sample CD.

Different Sounds for Different Styles

Before we begin, this is one simple and important point to make. Different styles of music call for different drum sounds. You will hear the variations of sounds and feel from each kit for the different styles for which they are used. For example, a loud cracking snare with a deep tone could be great for Rock, but not so great for a soft Jazz tune. Use your ears and judgment to use sound samples that work great for the style of music you are creating. There is no such thing as a "wrong" choice of sound, but if you're trying to obtain the "standard" sound for a certain style, then the grooves in this book and Audio Sample CD will be a great starting point for you.

Each groove chapter in this book is designed for a drum kit with the matching chapter title. Just like choosing your Dance Kit in Figure 1-8, you have the choice of the following drum kits:

- Rock Kit
- Metal Kit
- Dance Kit
- Funk Kit
- R&B Kit
- Jazz Kit
- World Kit

MIDI Map and Music Notation

Here is a comparison between standard music notation and the MIDI Maps you will be seeing in this book. In the next chapter, alongside every MIDI Map, music notation will be provided for a better understanding of what is happening rhythmically. As I said in the beginning, if you cannot read music notation, it is completely okay! By seeing the MIDI Maps and the music notation throughout this book, along with hearing the programmed grooves and the Audio Sample CD, you will slowly and naturally understand what you are seeing and hearing with both the MIDI Maps and musical notation.

The following is a diagram to introduce how the music notation and MIDI Maps are related, with simple beat divisions.

Whole Note

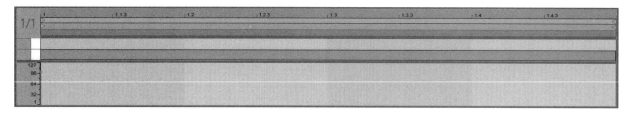

Figure 2-28

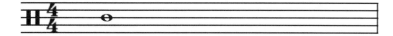

Figure 2-29

Half Notes

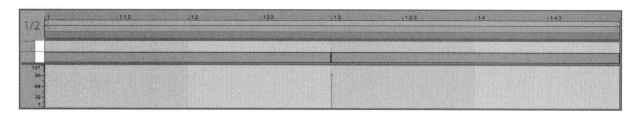

Figure 2-30

Figure 2-31

Quarter Notes

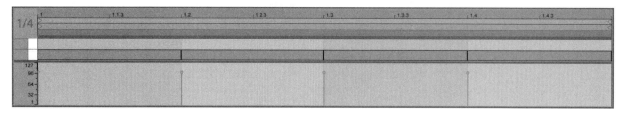

Figure 2-32

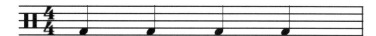

Figure 2-33

Eighth Notes

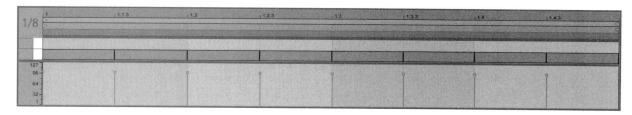

Figure 2-34

Figure 2-35

Eighth-Note Triplets

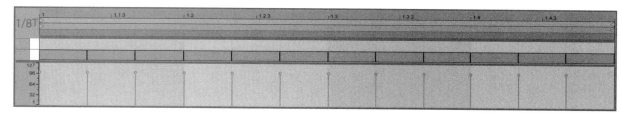

Figure 2-36

Figure 2-37

Sixteenth Notes

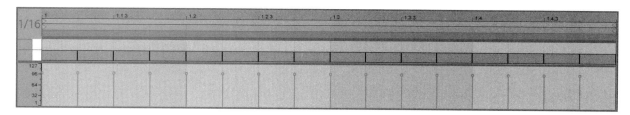

Figure 2-38

Figure 2-39

In the grooves throughout this book, you will see variations of the diagrams displayed in Figures 2-28 through 2-39. Feel free to refer to this page, for an understanding of what you are seeing in further chapters.

Here is a key that explains which drum sounds refer to the music notation in the next chapter.

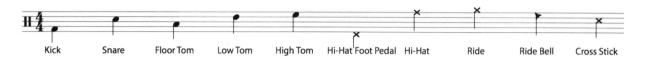

Kick   Snare   Floor Tom   Low Tom   High Tom   Hi-Hat Foot Pedal   Hi-Hat   Ride   Ride Bell   Cross Stick

Figure 2-40

Chapter **3**
GROOVES

How This Chapter Works

Each Page Has a Groove Title
This is the title of the style groove you will be programming.

Music Notation
Music notation is included with every groove for a quick and easy reference of the MIDI Map to music notation.

MIDI Map
The MIDI Map is the guide and road map for programming your MIDI data into Ableton Live's MIDI Note Editor.

Groove Tempo
This tempo references the BPM (beats per minute) of each groove's audio sample that's included on the DVD-ROM that accompanies this book.

An Explanation of the Groove
An explanation of each groove is included. This could include the groove's history, examples for real-life application (when, where, and why this groove would be applied), specific tips for programming, or a simple description of the groove.

The Grooves
It's time to bring everything together.

Eighth-Note Rock #1

Figure 3-1

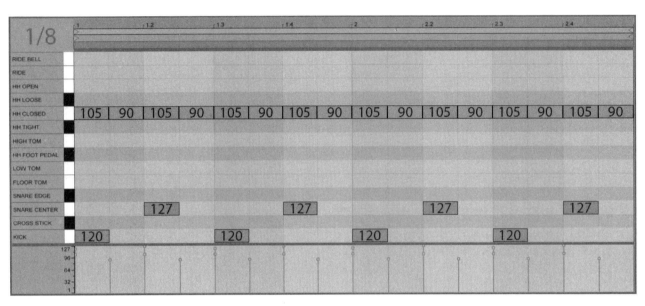

Figure 3-2

BPM: 120

This is the first variation of a basic Rock Groove. The kick drum is on beats 1 and 3, while the snare is on beats 2 and 4. The snare drum should carry this groove with a heavy backbeat, while the hi-hat is keeping time in eighth notes. Notice the rocking motion of the hi-hat; it's placing more emphasis on beats 1 and 3 to even out the dynamics in the groove against the heavy snare on beats 2 and 4. Follow the velocity changes as seen on the MIDI Map referring to this groove, to create dynamic range and a realistic and natural feel to maintain a groove and pocket for your programmed drums. Feel free to play around with the velocities until you have a sound you are comfortable with as well. Remember, there is no specific way to program a groove; use your ears as the final judge!

Eighth-Note Rock #2

Figure 3-3

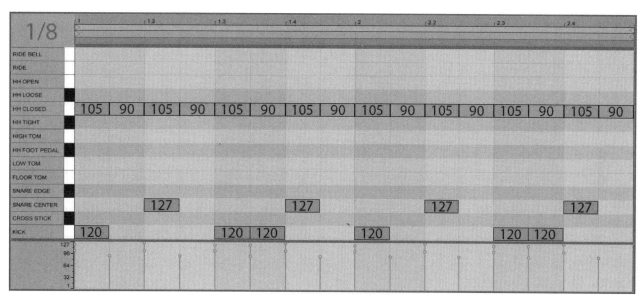

Figure 3-4

BPM: 120

Here is another variation of an eighth-note Rock Groove. One of the main roles of the kick drum is to emphasize the bass notes that are being played in a rhythm section. This famous Rock groove is created by adding an extra kick drum on the upbeat of beat 3 and could be used in many Rock playing situations, especially when the bassist is pedaling on an eighth-note pulse.

Eighth-Note Rock #3

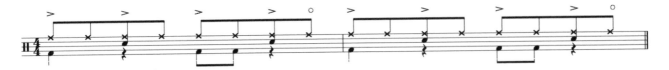

Figure 3-5

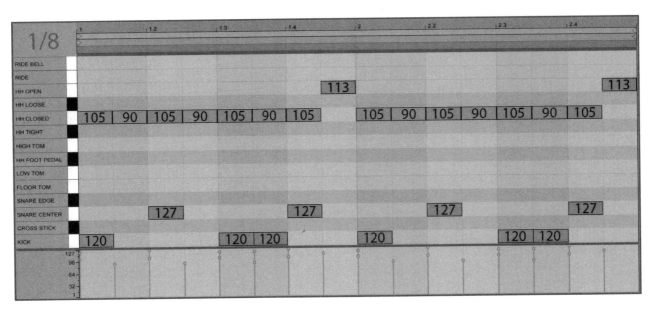

Figure 3-6

BPM: 120

This is where you could have fun with that hi-hat by taking the same groove as Eighth-Note Rock #2, adding the sound of an open hi-hat on the upbeat of beat 4, and the sound of a closed hi-hat on beat 1 of the next measure. This will create the sound of a hi-hat opening on the upbeat of beat 4 for half a beat, then closing up again on beat 1 to continue the groove.

Eighth-Note Rock #4

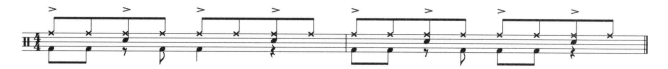

Figure 3-7

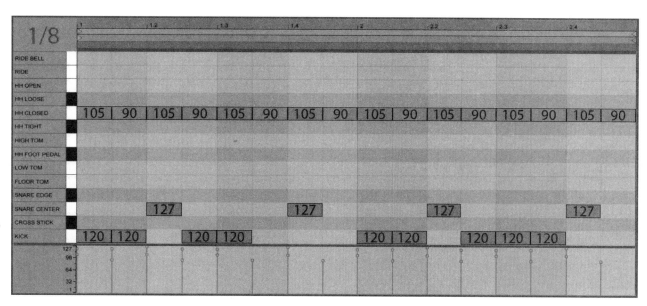

Figure 3-8

BPM: 120

Adding various kick drum patterns to a steady hi-hat and snare could add a great difference to the groove. Try out this pattern!

Eighth-Note Rock #5

Figure 3-9

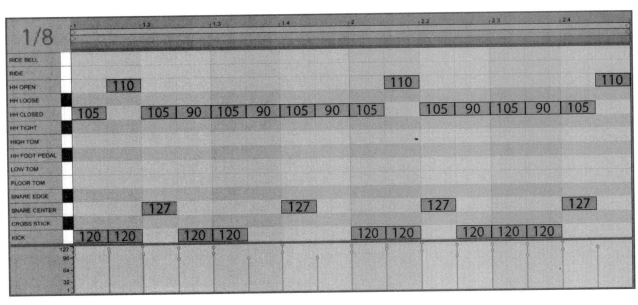

Figure 3-10

BPM: 120

Here is a variation of Eighth-Note Rock #4, with open hi-hats on various upbeats. Hear the difference of sound between the open hi-hat with the kick drum and without the kick drum? Those combinations of sounds could be used differently in many situations of playing and programming to achieve the sound desired. What is that desired sound, you ask? Well, it's up to you! The groove in Figure 3-10 is a guideline of where to start; use your ears to determine what sounds better to you and what sounds to explore next.

Eighth-Note Rock #6

Figure 3-11

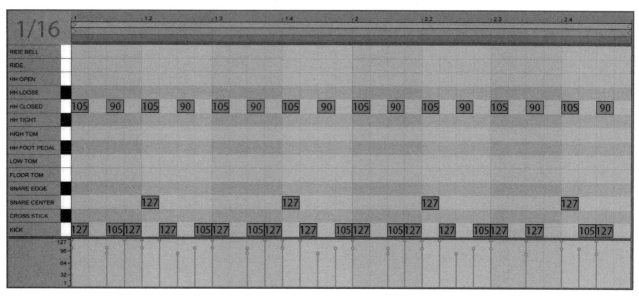

Figure 3-12

BPM: 115

This groove is a great example to show that the kick drum could have velocity changes as well. Doing this creates a "galloping" feel on the kick drum. Check it out! We also used a loose hi-hat sound to fill and thicken the sound of the eighth-note pulse of this groove.

Quarter-Note Rock #1

Figure 3-13

Figure 3-14

BPM: 120

This is the first Rock Groove where we will be playing quarter notes on the hi-hat. To fill the space and add some flavor to these types of grooves, using the sound of a loose hi-hat will do the trick for these quarter-note hi-hat hits that we want to ring out. The dirtier the hi-hat, the better. Remember, this is Rock!

Quarter-Note Rock #2

Figure 3-15

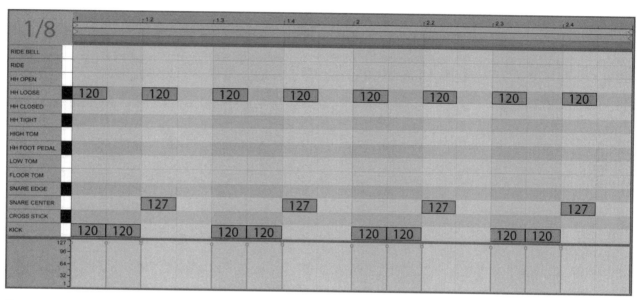

Figure 3-16

BPM: 120

Here is a variation of Quarter-Note Rock #1, with alternate kick drum hits.

Quarter-Note Rock #3

Figure 3-17

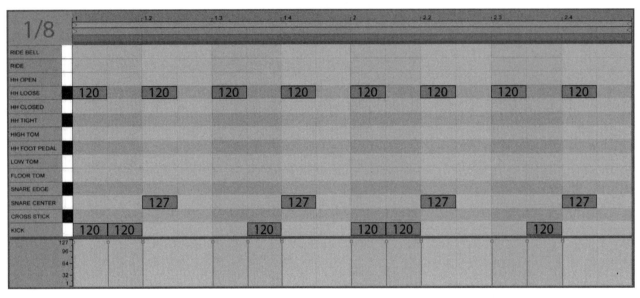

Figure 3-18

BPM: 170

Let's speed things up with this groove. At fast tempos, having quarter-note based grooves could help keep the groove feel relaxed and comfortable, not having it sound "rushed." The velocity of the open hi-hat is pretty constant; to create a heavy pulse for the groove, but changing the velocity slightly between hits could help make the cymbals sound more realistic and natural. This helps to replicate a human feel on the hi-hats, but remember not to overcompensate by creating too large of a velocity change between hits; keep them subtle to create a human-like feel with your programming. Once again, let your ears be the final judge.

Quarter-Note Rock #4

Figure 3-19

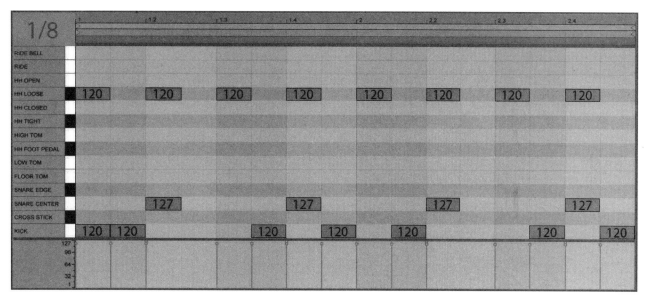

Figure 3-20

BPM: 170

Here is a variation of Quarter-Note Rock #3 with alternate kick drum hits. Another great way to emphasize the backbeat to this groove is to increase the velocity of the hi-hats on beats 2 and 4 to accent the snare drum. Feel free to mess around with the velocity to find some other cool and innovative variations.

Quarter-Note Rock #5

Figure 3-21

Figure 3-22

BPM: 170

This is a great groove, adding a feel of double time in the first half of the groove. An extra snare hit was added on beats 1 and 3 of measure 1 of the groove to create this feel. Try adding your own extra snare hits in the groove to create a new sound and feel!

Sixteenth-Note Rock #1

Figure 3-23

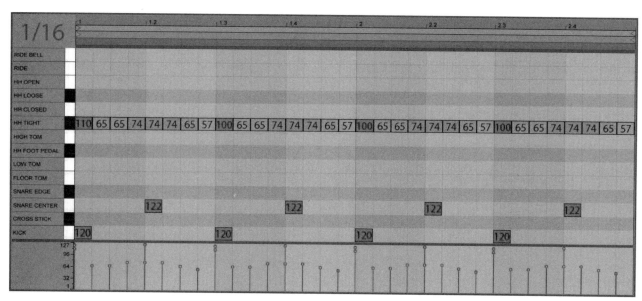

Figure 3-24

BPM: 115

Here is a variation of Eighth-Note Rock#1, but with sixteenth notes on the hi-hat. Notice the accents on the quarter notes to create a quarter-note pulse, while the sixteenth notes are filling in the space between. The velocity of every hi-hat hit is slightly different as well, to create more of a realistic sound and feel to the hi-hats. Try changing the velocities, not just for the hi-hat, but all of the sounds in the groove. You could end up with some real interesting results!

Sixteenth-Note Rock #2

Figure 3-25

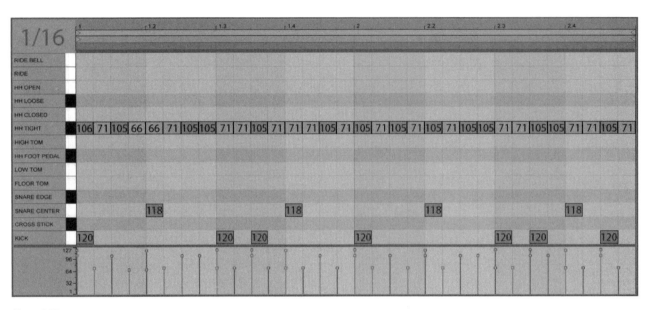

Figure 3-26

BPM: 115

In this groove, we're adding various accents on both the downbeats and upbeats of the hi-hat to create feel and motion within the groove. This groove could be considered a Hybrid Groove, which is incorporating feels of both Rock and Disco.

Sixteenth-Note Rock #3

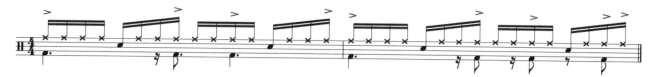

Figure 3-27

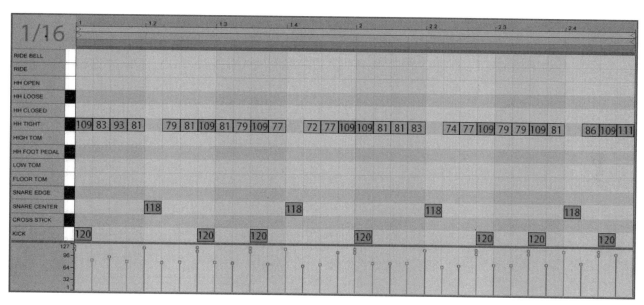

Figure 3-28

BPM: 115

Here is another variation of Sixteenth-Note Rock #1, with the use of kick drums on the upbeats to create syncopated rhythms within the groove, along with another element on the hi-hat to create a more human-like sound.

Here's the trick: At these faster tempos, most drummers cannot play the sixteenth notes on the hi-hat with only one hand; they have to alternate between the left and right hands. Because of this, most drummers do not play the hi-hat at the same time as the snare drum because they are alternating their hits between both of their hands. By removing a hi-hat sound for every snare hit, it replicates this sound.

Sixteenth-Note Rock #4

Figure 3-29

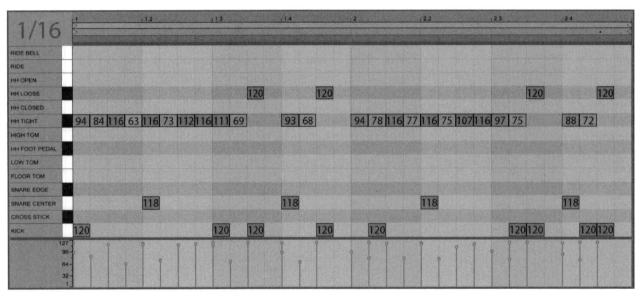

Figure 3-30

BPM: 115

Here is another variation of a sixteenth-note groove. Notice all of the velocity changes, to create that real feel groove!

Half-Time Rock #1

Figure 3-31

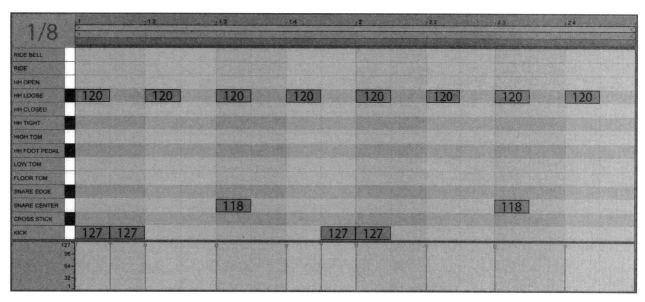

Figure 3-32

BPM: 115

Here is a half-time groove with an eighth-note hi-hat feel. To create this half-time feel, the snare backbeat is now on beat 3 instead of beats 2 and 4. This keeps the eighth-note pulse, but creates a laid-back feel to the groove.

Half-Time Rock #2

Figure 3-33

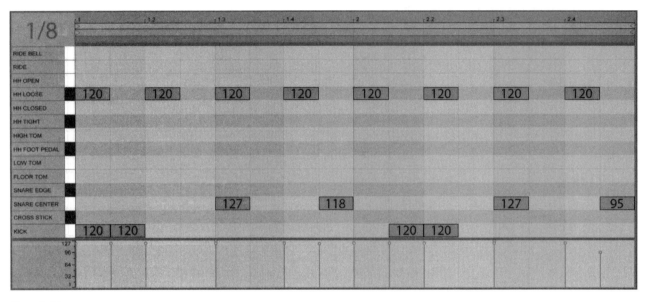

Figure 3-34

BPM: 115

An additional snare hit was added on the upbeat of beat 4 in measure 1, but keeping the heavy snare hit on beat 3 will help keep that backbeat for the half-time feel. Adding ghost notes within grooves can add some great realistic flavor. Ghost notes are notes played at lower velocities, to create the sound of a soft drum hit. I added one on the upbeat of beat 4 in measure 2. Try adding and moving around some snare ghost notes; they could really change the way a groove sounds!

Half-Time Rock #3

Figure 3-35

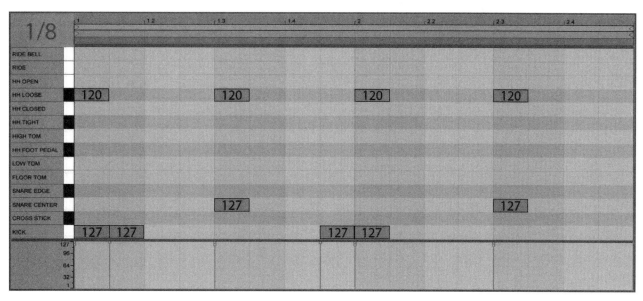

Figure 3-36

BPM: 115

Here is a slow and heavy half-time groove with a quarter-note feel. Hear the amount of space within this groove? A groove this simple could be used in many situations where you'd want to let the other instruments breathe and play more complex parts without any interference.

Half-Time Rock #4

Figure 3-37

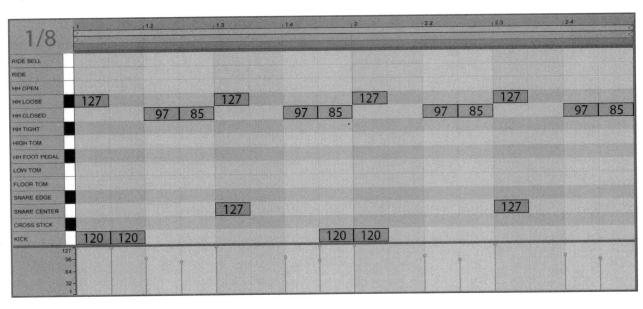

Figure 3-38

BPM: 130

Now, we're combining both quarter-note feels with eighth-note feels! The quarter-note hi-hats will all be playing open or loose hi-hat sounds, where the eighth-note hi-hats in between will play the closed hi-hat sounds, to create the sound that the hi-hat is being open and closed throughout the groove.

Half-Time Rock #5

Figure 3-39

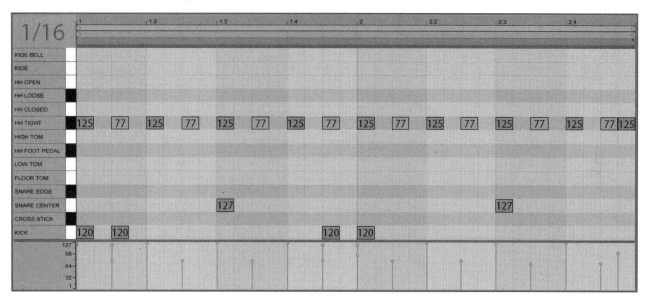

Figure 3-40

BPM: 130

Here, we are combining the eighth-note and sixteenth-note feels on the hi-hat at the end of measure 2. This is a great groove to use to connect the end of a phrase into another, with the small and precise sixteenth-note fill-like pattern on the hi-hat.

Half-Time Rock #6

Figure 3-41

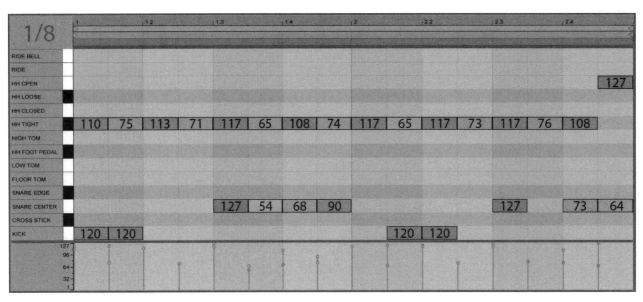

Figure 3-42

BPM: 130

Once again, those ghost notes are really adding some flavor to the groove. Here is an eighth-note feel variation that I enjoy to play with a half-time feel, and an open hi-hat on the upbeat of beat 4. Hear how the velocity increases in the snare's ghost notes from the upbeat of beat 3 until the upbeat of beat 4, in measure 1? There are lots of accents and velocity changes in this groove to create a really cool half-time feel.

Half-Time Rock #7

Figure 3-43

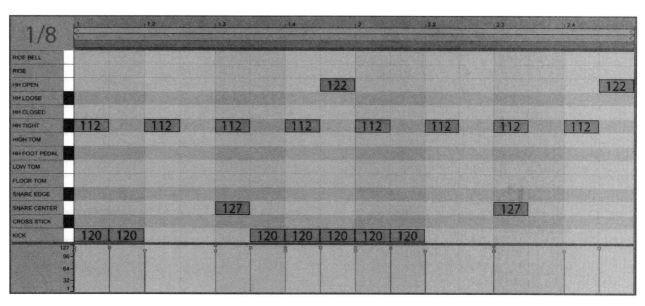

Figure 3-44

BPM: 130

This groove is the first where we've used a closed hi-hat sound for the quarter-note hi-hat hits. Sounds very clean and tight, right? Just because we're playing Rock, doesn't mean we have to re-create the sound of drums bashing and crashing as loud as possible. Precision and tightness are great tools when programming a Pop Rock drum groove for example. You can even experiment with all of the grooves from the Quarter-Note Rock Grooves and replace the open and loose hi-hats with closed hi-hats to hear the differences in tightness and precision.

Half-Time Rock #8

Figure 3-45

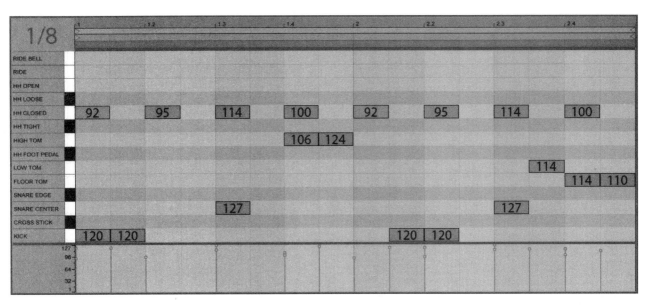

Figure 3-46

BPM: 130

This is where the grooves get really fun. Adding toms within a groove could add a great effect by incorporating the multiple sounds available in a drum kit.

Tom Rock #1

Figure 3-47

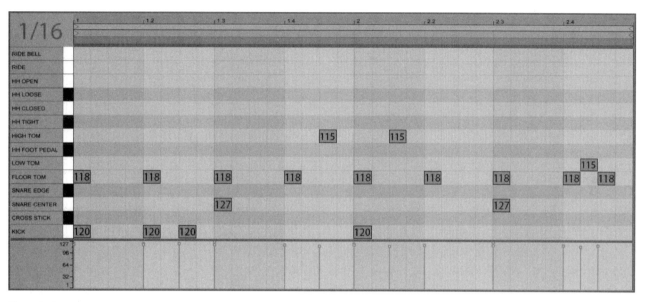

Figure 3-48

BPM: 135

This is the first groove where the main pulse and feel are relying on the toms of the drum kit. Here, we are taking a traditional half-time, quarter-note Rock pattern with the sound of the floor tom as the quarter-note pulse, along with adding various tom hits to fill up the groove. Tom-based grooves are a great way to add various sounds and textures to your drum grooves, while keeping a similar groove and structure to your drum programming. Try swapping the placement of the high toms and low toms to achieve a similar groove and feel, while applying a different sound to the groove.

Tom Rock #2

Figure 3-49

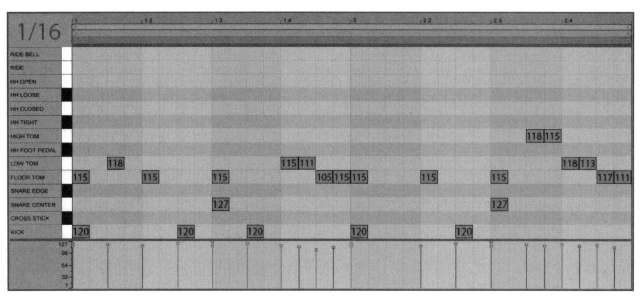

Figure 3-50

BPM: 135

Here is a trick with tom rolls, to make them sound more realistic. Notice the sixteenth-note roll at the end of the phrase. If you are programming rolls across toms, by lowering the velocity slightly on the second hit of the same tom, this creates the effect of a drummer using his or her right and left hand. Even the greatest drummers with the most precise sticking have these slight changes, and there is most likely a sound difference between the actual drumsticks as well. It's not a big thing to notice, but it will add great realism to your tom rolls, and keep them from sounding "robotic."

Tom Rock #3

Figure 3-51

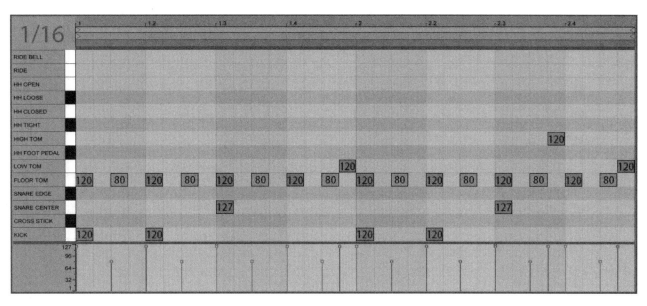

Figure 3-52

BPM: 130

This groove is a great example of using your velocity to enhance the groove with dynamics. By adding an accent on the floor tom on every quarter note, it creates a "rocking" feel to the eighth-note groove.

Tom Rock #4

Figure 3-53

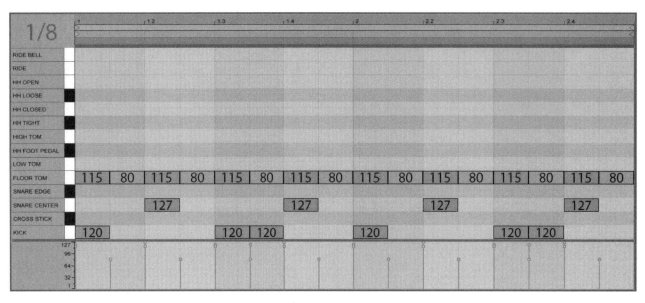

Figure 3-54

BPM: 127

This groove is using the same "rocking" feel on the floor tom, but now with the snare on beats 2 and 4. Hear how the placement of the snare can change the feel of the groove?

Tom Rock #5

Figure 3-55

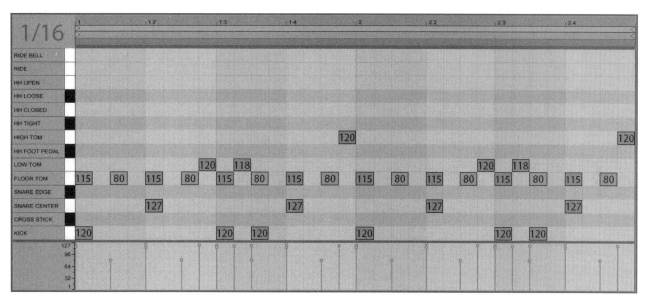

Figure 3-56

BPM: 127

Here is a variation of Tom Rock #4, with various tom hits to fill up the groove.

Tom Rock #6

Figure 3-57

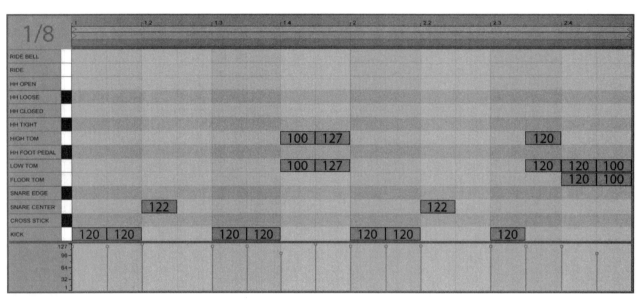

Figure 3-58

BPM: 127

Here is that classic '80s Rock groove that works as a great fill as well! Try this heavy tom-oriented groove as a transition from one groove to another.

Tom Rock #7

Figure 3-59

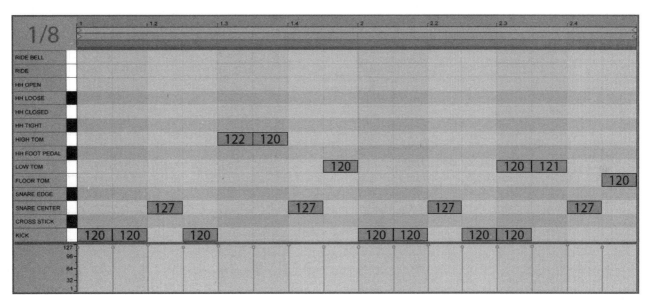

Figure 3-60

BPM: 127

Here is a variation of Tom Rock #6

Fast Tom Rock #1

Figure 3-61

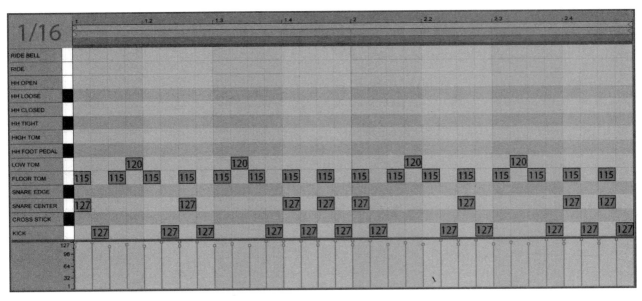

Figure 3-62

BPM: 120

By alternating the floor tom and the kick drum every sixteenth note, you create this great "double bass drum" sound that adds excitement, speed, and energy to a Rock groove for those fast and heavy songs!

Fast Tom Rock #2

Figure 3-63

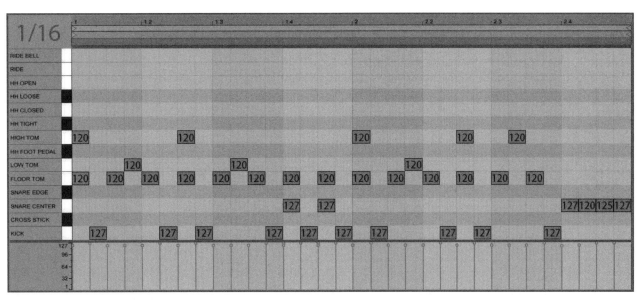

Figure 3-64

BPM: 120
Variation of Fast Tom Rock #1

Fast Tom Rock #3

Figure 3-65

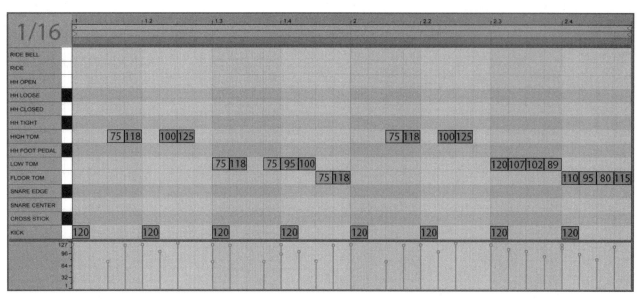

Figure 3-66

BPM: 120

In this groove, by keeping the quarter-note pulse on the kick drum; you are laying down a straight groove, allowing freedom to layer a rhythmic pattern on top of the quarter-note pulse. Try programming various patterns over the steady kick drum for new results!

Metal #1

Figure 3-67

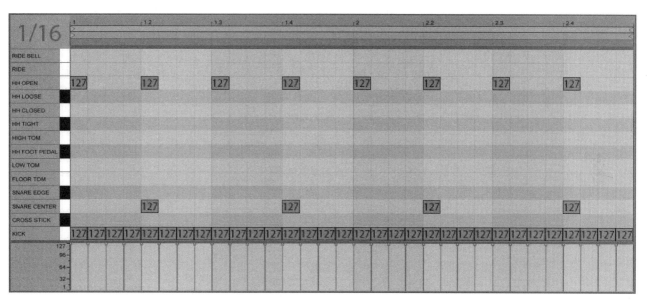

Figure 3-68

BPM: 135

This is a basic sixteenth-note double bass drum groove. The open hi-hat sound playing on the quarter notes creates this large, open, heavy-sounding pulse while the snare plays the backbeat on beats 2 and 4. This groove is great for Metal programming, at slow or fast tempos.

Metal #2

Figure 3-69

Figure 3-70

BPM: 135

Here is a kick drum variation groove of Metal #1.

Metal #3

Figure 3-71

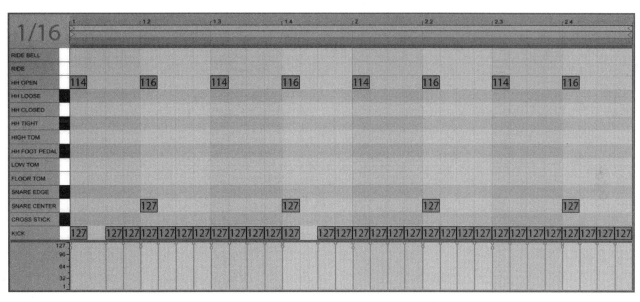

Figure 3-72

BPM: 135

Here is a kick drum variation groove of Metal #1.

Metal #4

Figure 3-73

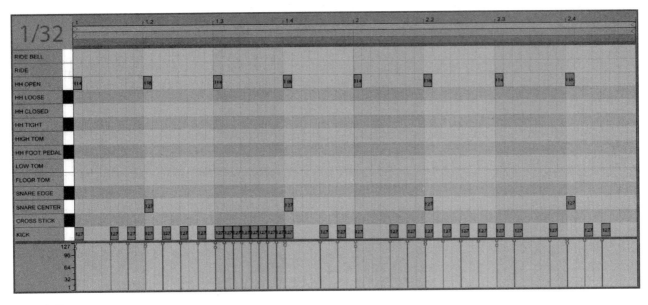

Figure 3-74

BPM: 135

Here is a kick drum variation groove of Metal #1, with the use of thirty-second-note kick drums—wow that is fast! I'm glad we're programming this one!

Metal #5

Figure 3-75

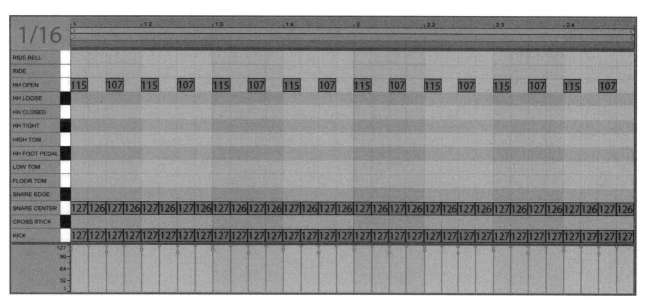

Figure 3-76

BPM: 135

Here is that famous blast beat groove wanted for those fast Metal phrases! Hear the accents on the snare drum on the eighth notes? While playing sixteenth notes on the snare drum, the eighth notes are being accented to create that "rocking" motion once again, ending up with a more realistic sound and feel.

Metal #6

Figure 3-77

Figure 3-78

BPM: 135

Here is a variation of Metal #5, with various accents on the snare drum.

Metal #7

Figure 3-79

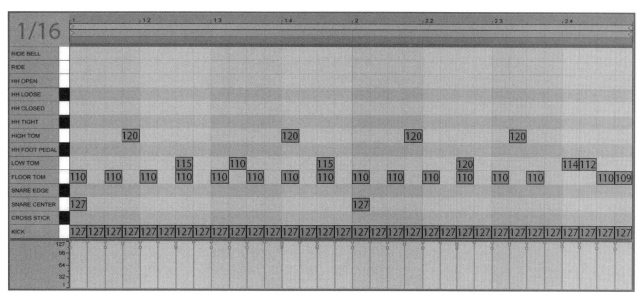

Figure 3-80

BPM: 130

Here is a tom-oriented groove, while keeping straight sixteenth notes on the kick drum.

Metal #8

Figure 3-81

Figure 3-82

BPM: 130

Once again, here is another classic Metal groove. Even though a steady sixteenth-note pattern is applied on the kick drum, the snare and floor tom are accenting every quarter note to bring out a heavy downbeat.

Metal #9

Figure 3-83

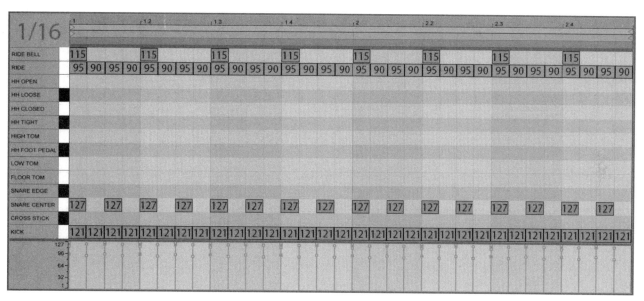

Figure 3-84

BPM: 130

This is a great groove in the programming world because, if you were on a real kit, you would need five limbs to play it! While the kick drum and ride cymbal are playing a straight sixteenth-note pattern, the snare drum is playing an eighth-note pattern with accents on the quarter note for a "rocking" feel, and to top off this heavy Metal groove, the ride bell is added on top to accent the quarter notes of the groove, Super-Heavy-Groove.

Metal #10

Figure 3-85

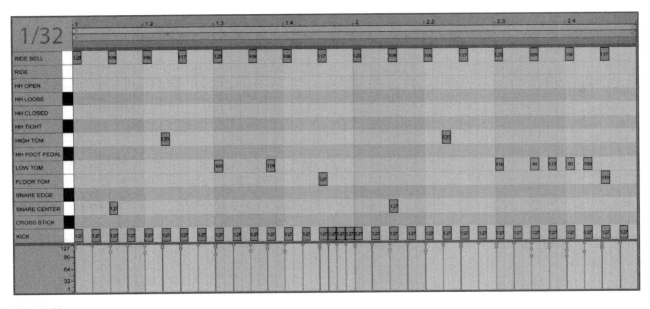

Figure 3-86

BPM: 125

This groove is a great mix of all the Metal grooves together, to show what could be done by experimenting with your programming skills. Try mixing and matching all of the previous grooves to create something new for yourself!

Dance #1

Figure 3-87

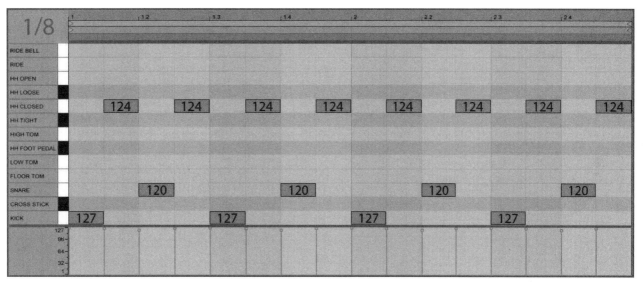

Figure 3-88

BPM: 125

Here is a classic Disco groove that is great for all styles of music, when you want to incorporate a simple but powerful groove with feel into your music. You'll notice that in all of the dance grooves in this book, a constant quarter-note bass drum will be underneath and driving the beat, with various hi-hat and snare drum patterns.

Dance #2

Figure 3-89

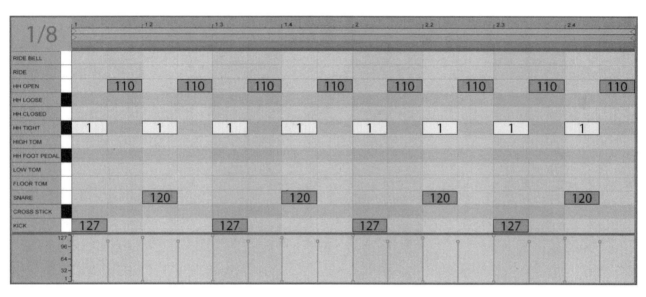

Figure 3-90

BPM: 125

In this variation, the sound of an open hi-hat is being played on the upbeat of the quarter note. The closed hi-hat sound is being programmed to choke the sound of the open hi-hat, but we'll keep it at a low velocity so it is inaudible.

Dance #3

Figure 3-91

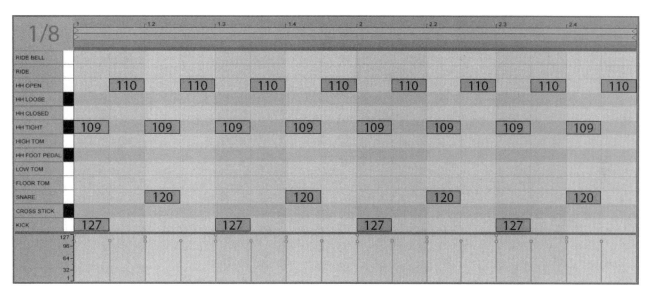

Figure 3-92

BPM: 125

This is a great variation of Dance #2, where the closed hi-hat is playing the downbeat, and the open hi-hat is playing the upbeat. This simulates the sound of a drummer hitting the top of the hi-hat with the tip of the stick on the downbeats, where the shoulder of the stick hits the open hi-hat on the upbeats, creating hi-hat accents on the upbeat of this groove.

Dance #4

Figure 3-93

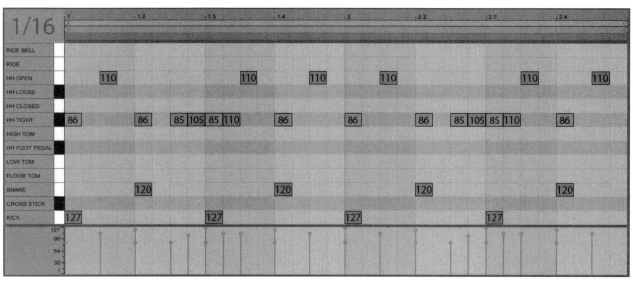

Figure 3-94

BPM: 125

Here is another Disco groove variation, with various accents and rhythms on the closed hi-hat; in between the open hi-hat hits on the upbeats. This could be used to fill space within the groove, as well as leading into new groove variations, when applied at the end of a groove, similar to the idea used in Half-Time Rock #5.

Dance #5

Figure 3-95

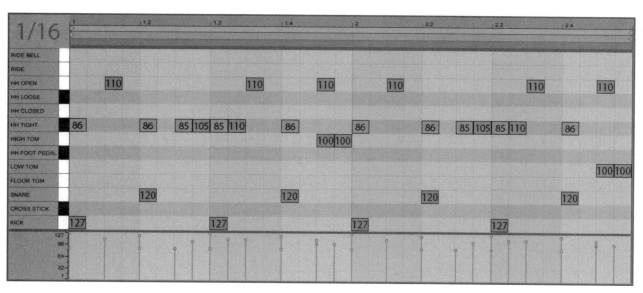

Figure 3-96

BPM: 125

This is a variation of Dance #4; adding tom hits on the upbeat of beat 4.

Dance #6

Figure 3-97

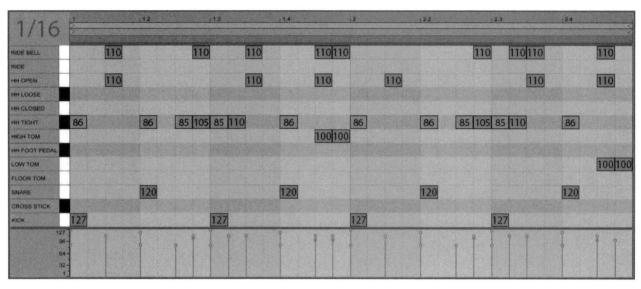

Figure 3-98

BPM: 125

The shoulder of a drumstick hitting the ride of the bell is a great sound; let's add some rhythmic bell patterns to Dance #5! As you have seen, from Dance #4 to Dance #6, various rhythms and sounds were being layered on top of the steady groove. This layering system works great for grooves with a simple underlying pulse. Try incorporating sounds from previous groove examples, to layer onto your dance grooves!

Funk #1

Figure 3-99

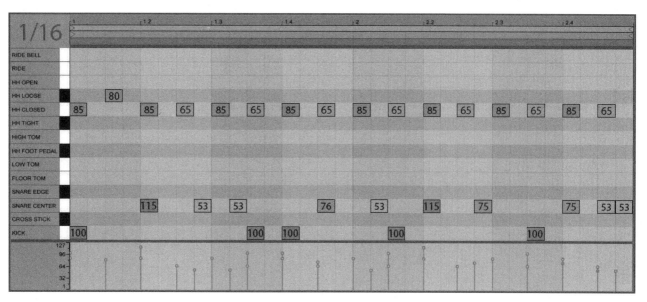

Figure 3-100

BPM: 115

Here is a style where we will be moving the velocity marker around a lot! Funk Grooves are full of ghost notes and accents all over the drum kit, so knowing where to apply these velocity changes, while programming in this style, is crucial to obtain a natural groove and pocket. Follow the MIDI Map in Figure 3-100 as a starting point for these grooves, and then take it from there!

Funk #2

Figure 3-101

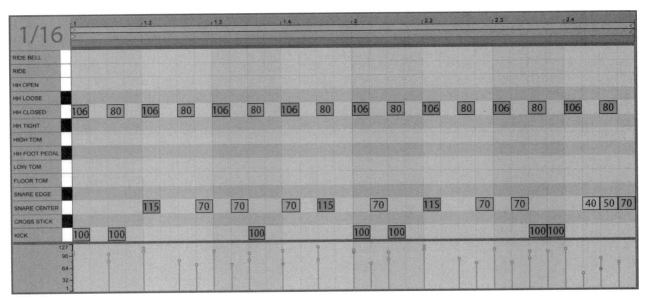

Figure 3-102

BPM: 115

Notice the accented snare is not always on beats 2 and 4, or on 1 and 3 anymore. Misplacing the beat is a great thing to do in this style, while maintaining the groove and pocket as well. Also, hear those snare ghost notes at the end of the second measure? They're slightly increasing in volume, to bring you back into the phrase and create a slightly more natural feel. Try it out!

Funk #3

Figure 3-103

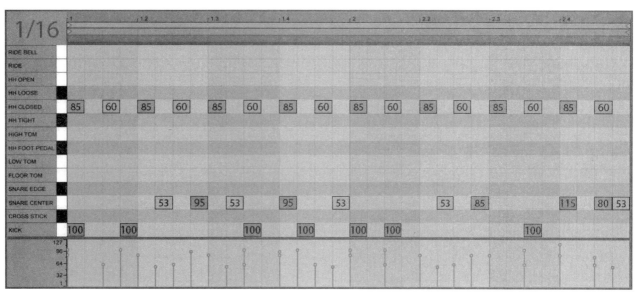

Figure 3-104

BPM: 110

Like Funk #2, this variation is very interesting because of the misplacement of the snare drum. As in the previous Funk Grooves as well, notice the steady hi-hat. Even though the snare drum is very free with its movement and accents, the hi-hat is very straight with consistent accents throughout the groove.

Funk #4

Figure 3-105

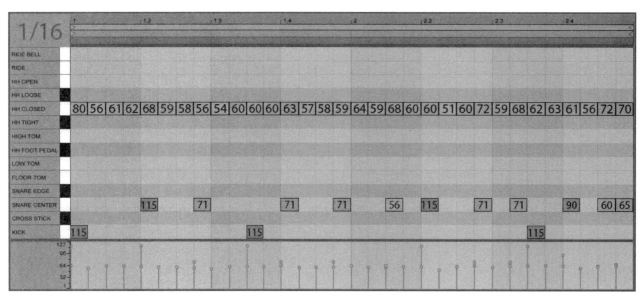

Figure 3-106

BPM: 100

This sixteenth-note groove is a classic Funk groove from the late '60s. The trick to this hi-hat sound is to capture a straight sixteenth-note hi-hat pulse with no accents, but to add your own slight variations of velocity to obtain a real-feel sound to the hi-hat's groove.

Funk #5

Figure 3-107

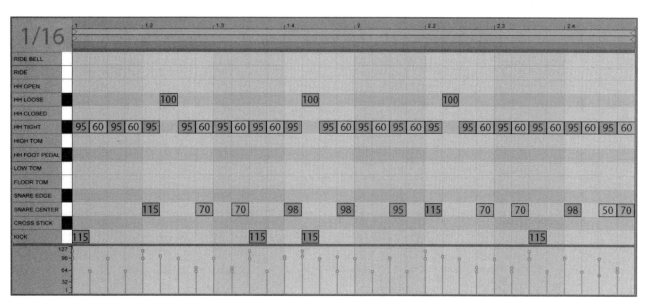

Figure 3-108

BPM: 105

This is another famous Funk Groove from the late '60s with the use of the open hi-hat sound on various beats.

R&B #1

Figure 3-109

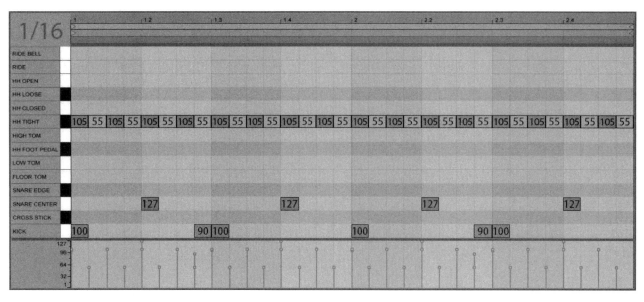

Figure 3-110

BPM: 90

This sixteenth-note groove has a straight hi-hat accenting each eighth note, to create a smooth rocking motion. The kick drum and snare drum are both at high velocity to accent the quarter note. Notice the velocity on the kick drum is higher on the downbeat to accent that pulse.

R&B #2

Figure 3-111

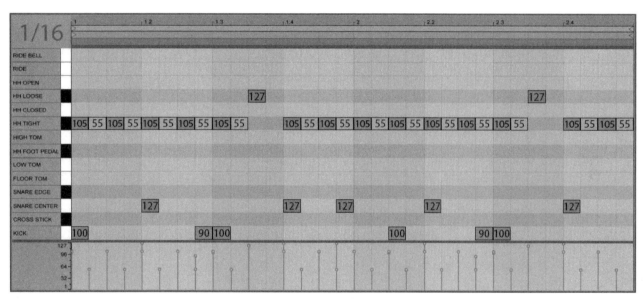

Figure 3-112

BPM: 95

Here is another variation with the sound of an open hi-hat on the upbeat of beat 3. Hear how the open hi-hat is sustained until the downbeat of beat 4? Leaving the open space creates great effect in a slow open groove like this one. Also notice how all of the snares are very powerful and at high velocities. In a groove like this one, having a loud cracking snare to reinforce the backbeat is very essential. There are no set rules, though. Feel free to add ghost notes in a groove similar to this one; it could add great effect to the sound!

R&B #3

Figure 3-113

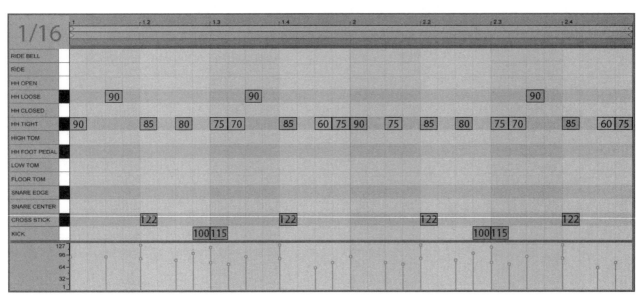

Figure 3-114

BPM: 90

Here is a groove that sounds different from the other R&B Grooves played. What might sound off is the kick drum. Most people are used to hearing the downbeat on beat 1 with the kick drum, where in this case, the kick drum isn't until the sixteenth note before beat 2. This is a great groove example, because it shows that there are many places to place a kick drum. It doesn't always have to be the start to a groove on the downbeat of beat 1. Try moving the kick drum around to various placements; you will most likely find new groove variations you've never thought about programming.

R&B #4

Figure 3-115

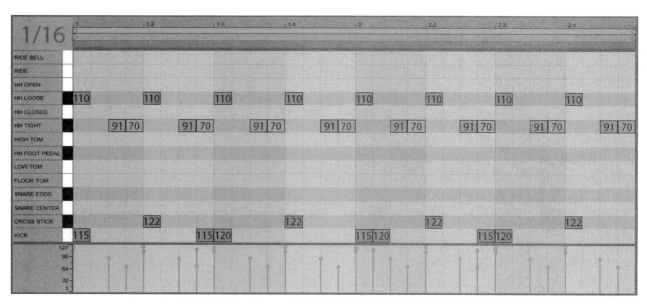

Figure 3-116

BPM: 90

Here is a groove with open hi-hat sounds as the quarter-note pulse with sixteenth-note closed hi-hats in between. Like in R&B #2, notice how there is a gap between the open hi-hat until the next closed hi-hat sound; they are not following each other right on the sixteenth-note grid. Once again, this helps create space in the groove, especially in an example like this, where there is a lot going on. A cross stick sound is being used on the snare, but this groove would also work great with a loud rim shot crack, or soft snare hit as well to enforce that backbeat. Use your ears to determine what sound to use for the tune needed.

R&B #5

Figure 3-117

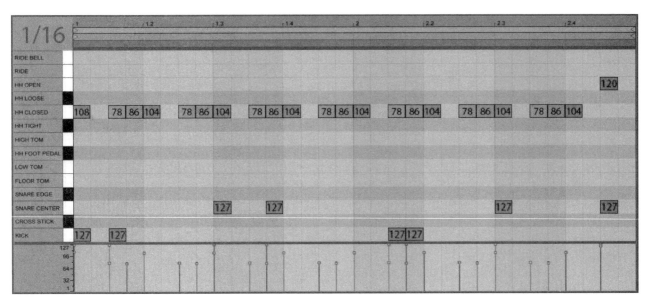

Figure 3-118

BPM: 105

This groove has a similar hi-hat pattern to R&B #4, but instead of the open hi-hat sound enforcing the quarter note, the accented closed hi-hat is doing the job. Notice the slight velocity changes on the hi-hat to create a human-like feel and sound. This is a great half-time groove to play on various styles of music such as R&B, Rock, or Hip Hop.

Jazz Grooves

We are now entering the Jazz drum programming world. Jazz in particular is a challenging but amazing style of music to program, not just because of the dynamic changes and realistic feel to obtain, but also because of the freedom within the style, which is continually expanding to this day. In this chapter, you will learn how to create a realistic swinging Jazz feel, bass drum and snare drum comping patterns, and reasons to use these patterns throughout a tune.

Jazz Feel Example: Unlike most American music, Jazz is felt in triplets, creating a swing feel. To create this sound, your MIDI Map will be set to a triplet grid instead of a straight grid.

- Simply right-click on the MIDI Note Editor to bring up the pop-up menu and click on Triplet Grid.

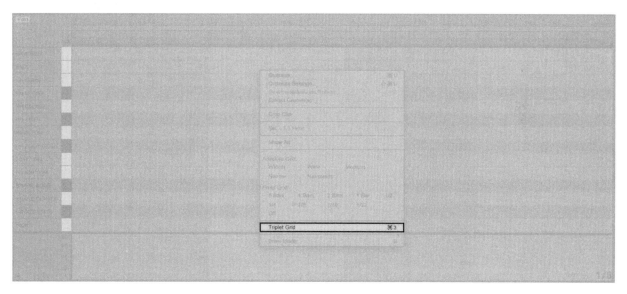

Figure 3-119

- You will see in the bottom right corner that the Marker Snap has changed from 1/8 to 1/8T

Figure 3-120

You are now in an eighth-note triplet grid.
Follow the MIDI Map in Figure 3-121 to create a Jazz ride pattern.

NOTE: Play the following example at 125 BPM.

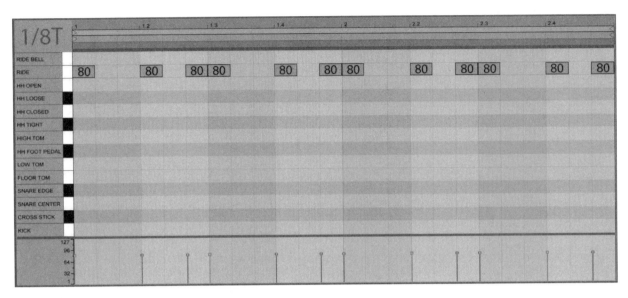

Figure 3-121

Notice the placement of the ride cymbal's MIDI Notes to create that swinging Jazz ostinato. The hi-hat in Jazz is used as a time keeper which is mostly kept on beats 2 and 4 to keep the drive in the groove.

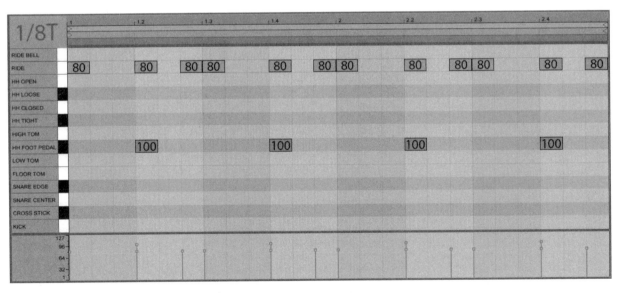

Figure 3-122

Now that we have the placement of the ride and hi-hat, let's make it sound more like a natural swinging groove!

- Create accents on beats 2 and 4 of the ride cymbal by raising the velocity; this will help drive the groove. Follow the slight velocity changes on the MIDI Map referring to Figure 3-123 as well, to create a more realistic vibe on the ride cymbal.

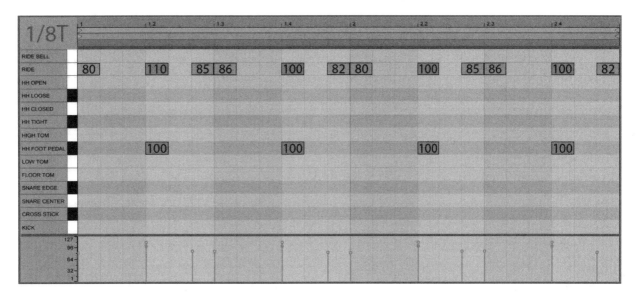

Figure 3-123

Remember to keep beats 2 and 4 accented to drive the groove, but also note that there are no rules about where to accent the ride in Jazz. Use your ears to determine where it is best to place those accents along with the music. The following examples provide a great starting point for your Jazz programming.

Jazz #1

Figure 3-124

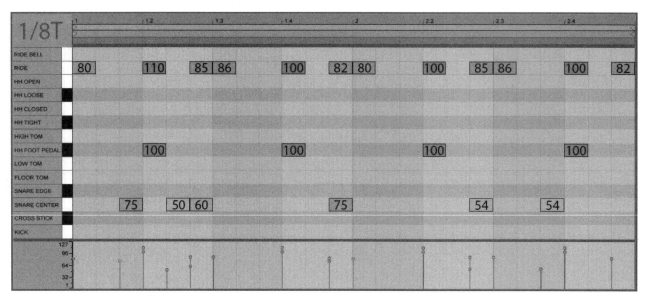

Figure 3-125

BPM: 130

This is the first Jazz groove that we will be programming. Notice the snare drum in this groove is at a very low velocity to create ghost notes throughout the groove. In Jazz-style drumming, the snare drum is a great tool for comping, which accompanies or complements the ride cymbal pattern as well as the band. Snare drum comping patterns could be used to emphasize specific phrases of a tune, accompany a soloist, and even more. Try this groove out as your first snare drum comping pattern.

Jazz #2

Figure 3-126

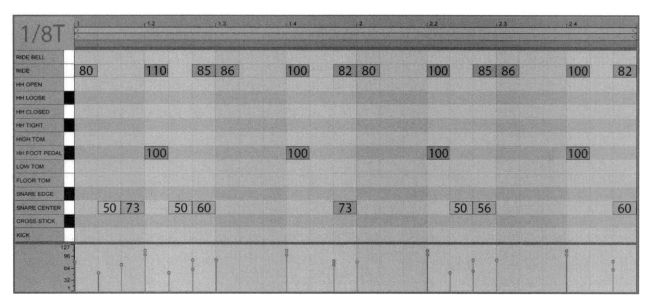

Figure 3-127

BPM: 130

Here is another snare comping pattern, with a standard swing groove.

Jazz #3

Figure 3-128

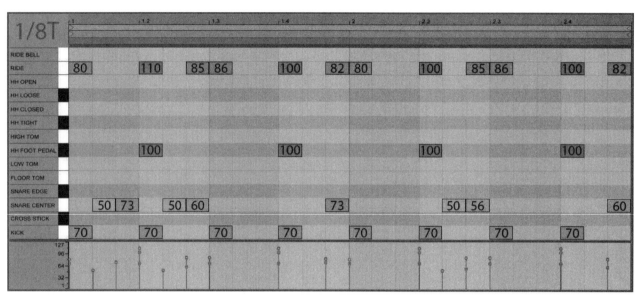

Figure 3-129

BPM: 130

Here is a variation of Jazz #2, but with a quarter-note driven bass drum at a low velocity. This is also known as "feathering" the kick.

Jazz #4

Figure 3-130

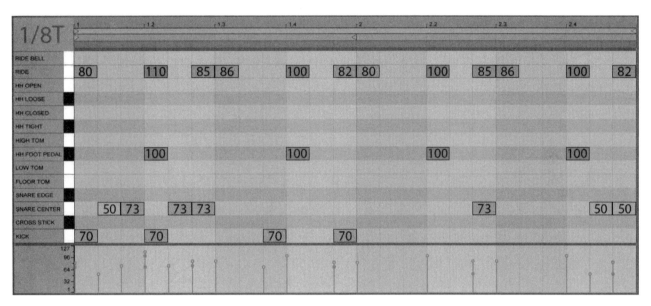

Figure 3-131

BPM: 130

Here is a pattern with both snare drum and bass drum comping.

Jazz #5

Figure 3-132

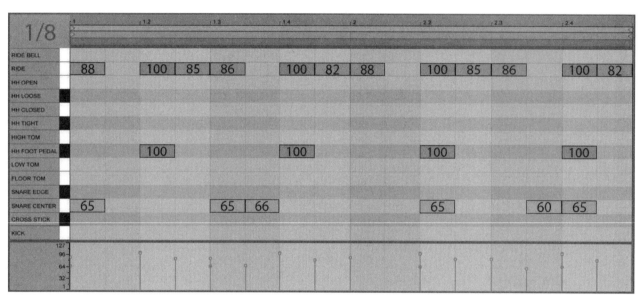

Figure 3-133

BPM: 260

At faster tempos, the swing feel in Jazz starts to straighten it's self out. Notice how the MIDI Map is set back to an eighth-note straight grid. The accents on the ride are still on beats 2 and 4, as well as the foot closed hi-hat.

Jazz #6

Figure 3-134

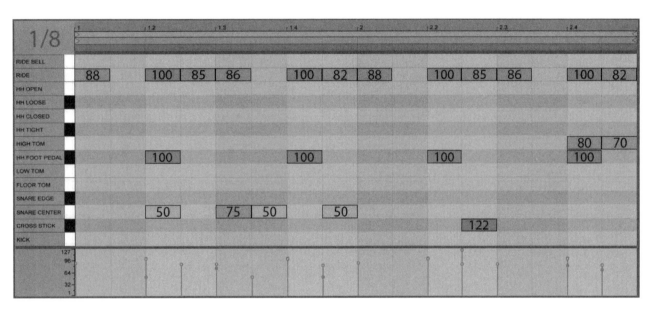

Figure 3-135

BPM: 260

Various sounds could be added to these Jazz grooves as well. In this example, the sound of a snare cross stick and tom were added into the groove. Try adding some sounds and variations of your own to create some interesting new Jazz grooves!

Jazz #7

Figure 3-136

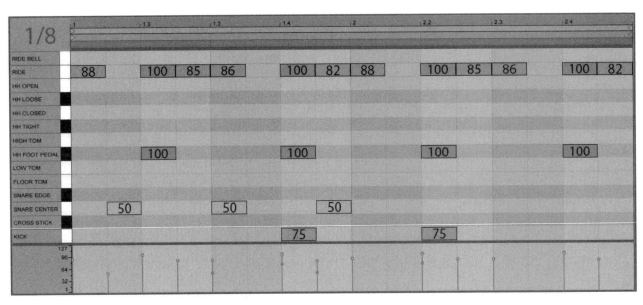

Figure 3-137

BPM: 260

Here is another comping variation of an up-tempo Jazz groove.

Jazz #8

Figure 3-138

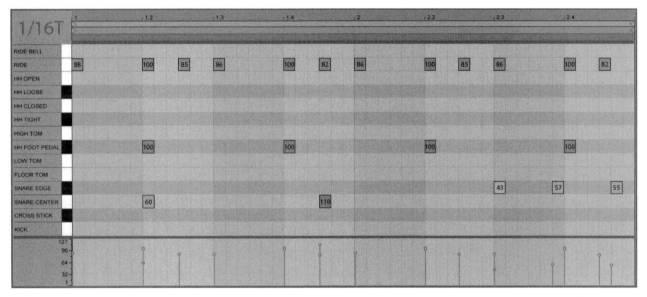

Figure 3-139

BPM: 260

Here is another snare comping pattern, with the use of quarter-note triplets in the second bar. This is also the first groove where we are using the sound of the snare edge. Try throwing it in some other grooves as ghost notes, for a new effect!

World Grooves

Before we get started in this section, there is something very important to be said about this style of music for the drum kit. The American drum kit that we will be using to program these World Grooves was not around when all of these grooves were invented. These are multipercussion parts that we're adapting for the drum kit. For example, the snare drum could be re-creating a timbale part; the toms could be conga and bongo parts; the ride bell could replace a cowbell, and many more. This being said, if you are producing or arranging an Afro Cuban track with a part being played by a percussionist, take into consideration that you could be doubling various percussion parts with the drum kit that could possibly be distracting or interrupting within the rhythm section. By listening to more World music and becoming familiar with the feel and sound, you will understand what percussive instruments are being adapted to the drum kit. The next 11 grooves have a wide variety of sounds, rhythms, and programming tips that you will really enjoy. Many of these styles and tips could be used in previous grooves to create your own Hybrid Grooves.

The information provided with the following World grooves is breaching the tip of the styles history. Each one of these World grooves is worth a full study of its own, so don't let this book be the end of your adventure for these grooves. There are many ways to find information about these styles, such as books, classes, Internet sources, and specifically live performances, to see, hear, and feel this music in person. These topics are very interesting, and I encourage you to explore the following styles' history and application to present-day performance, which would only benefit your World groove programming.

Calypso

Figure 3-140

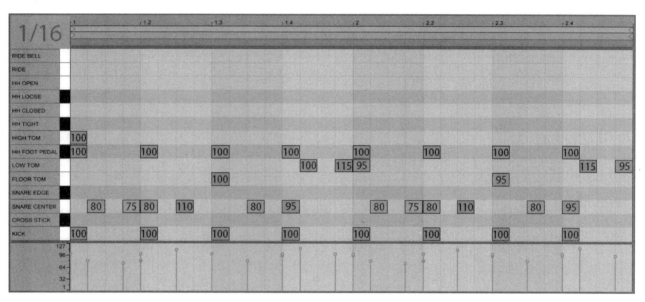

Figure 3-141

BPM: 120

Here is a great groove from the Caribbean that is not only fun to play, but also to program! Because these World grooves are so fragile and natural to the ear, we do not want to take those characteristics away from them while programming. There are many changes in velocity throughout this groove to keep the natural sound of the drums, as well as the pocket. The accented side stick on the upbeat of beat 2, and the accented rack tom on the upbeat of beat 4 are examples of where those velocities should be at a higher level, to really bring out that accent. Decreasing velocities at the end of a phrase will also help bring a push and pull wave motion throughout the groove to help with the natural dynamic feel.

Soca

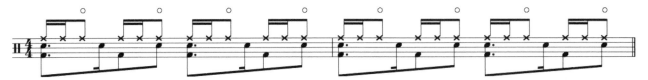

Figure 3-142

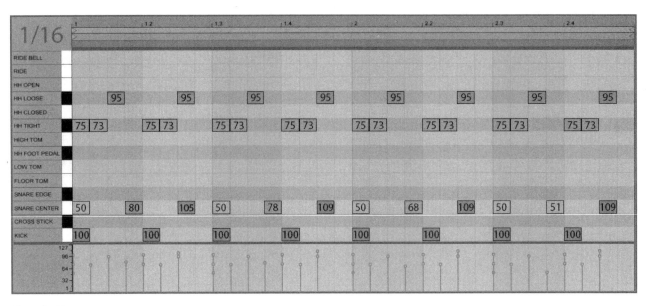

Figure 3-143

BPM: 115

Like the Calypso, the Soca will keep a "four-on-the-floor kick drum," meaning there is a kick drum pulse on every quarter note, as well as the similar feel of accenting the upbeats, but now with the snare drum and hi-hat. This is a groove with many sounds and velocity differences, so using the MIDI Map in Figure 3-143 as a starting point should be a great help. Definitely feel free to play around with the velocities and ghost notes in the groove, to create something of your own afterwards!

Bossa Nova

Figure 3-144

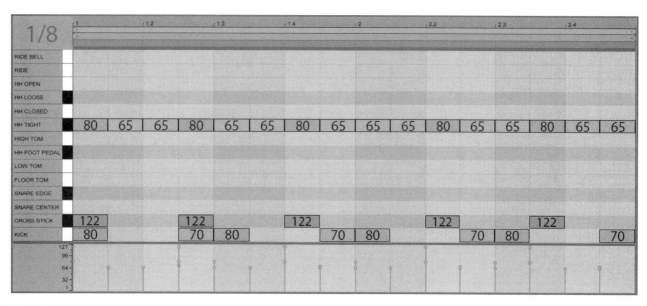

Figure 3-145

BPM: 117

This Brazilian groove has a gentle feel, with the intension of creating space and softness. Notice the velocity changes in this groove; the levels are very low and the changes between each hit are very subtle. The downbeats of the kick drum have a slightly higher velocity to create the feel of an accent on beats 1 and 3, as well as bring motion and feel to the groove. The closed hi-hat and side stick sounds are both at low velocities, with subtle changes throughout the groove to create more of a human feel. Another great variation of this groove would be to have the ride cymbal keep the eighth-note pulse instead of the closed hi-hat. The ride cymbal adds a soft legato feel to the groove, but remember to keep the velocity at a low level to obtain that feel. Adding velocity changes to the ride cymbal, to create accents along with the side stick Bossa Nova pattern could add to the groove as well, and be a great starting point to figure out where to add your own accents to embellish the groove.

Samba

Figure 3-146

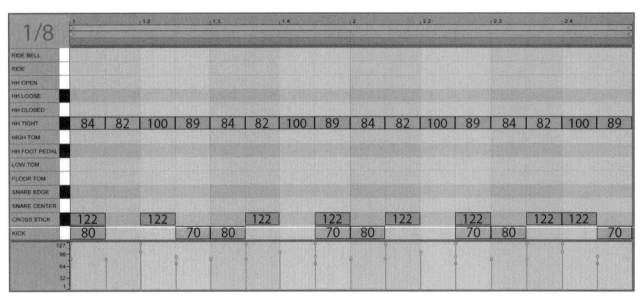

Figure 3-147

BPM: 120

This is another Brazilian groove that has a similar kick drum pattern to the Bossa Nova. The kick drum will act as a pulse for the groove, and here's a great trick to make the kick drum sound even more real. Adding kick drum accents by increasing the velocity to beats 1 and 3 will help with a more human-like feel on the kick. Now bring up the velocity of the kick drum on beat 3 to add a heavier feel to the second half of the bar. This will help even out the groove's feel as well as create a human-like touch to the kick drum as it would be played on a real kit for a Samba pattern. The bell pattern is also a standard part of this groove, while keeping a constant foot closed hi-hat sound on beats 2 and 4. The toms and side stick are there to embellish the groove and add flavor. Feel free to create new tom, side stick, and snare patterns over the sounds of the kick drum, bell pattern, and hi-hat of the samba!

Fast Samba

Figure 3-148

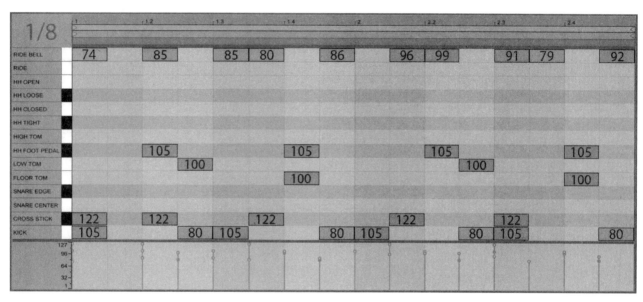

Figure 3-149

BPM: 210
Here is an up-tempo variation of the Samba

Merengue

Figure 3-150

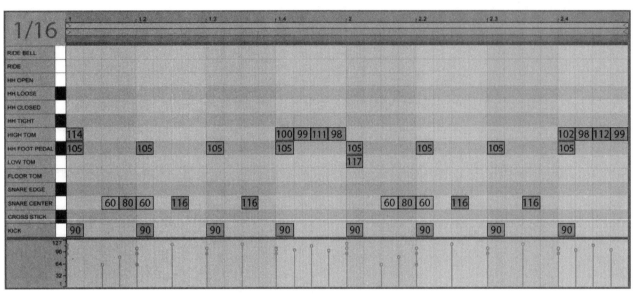

Figure 3-151

BPM: 145

This is a Dominican groove, which is meant for high energy and a fast driving motion. The sound of the kick drum and foot closed hi-hat keeps a quarter-note pulse, to push this groove. For this example, the sounds of the snare drum, in this case, are the sounds of the tip of the stick on the skin, playing soft and fast ghost notes as well as rim shots on the upbeats. The toms are the fun part to program in this groove. Notice the velocity changes on the toms. Because this groove has such a natural feel and energy to it, we don't want to ruin that with a robotic "machine gun" tom roll on every fourth beat. To do this we will use a great velocity technique that will be used to alternate the velocity up and down slightly, to re-create the sound of a drummer using the right and left hand. We do not want it to be overexaggerated and throw the groove off, but just enough to get rid of that robotic tom roll that would be heard in a classic shooter video game. Try this technique out for various rolls around the toms on the entire kit as well!

Cha-Cha

Figure 3-152

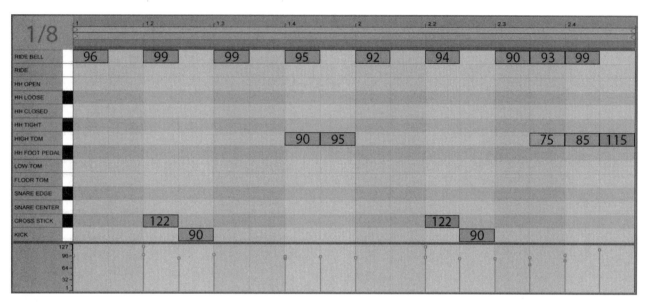

Figure 3-153

BPM: 130

This is a great and simple Afro Cuban groove that works well in slow and medium tempos. This groove is meant to have a quarter-note based cowbell pattern, which in this example will be played on the bell of the ride cymbal. Having a constant velocity for the bell pattern can really help set the drive and pace for this groove, although we will keep it slightly varied to create a natural feel. The kick drum pattern is also something that could be played around with in this groove. A standard Cha-Cha has a kick drum on the upbeat of beat 2 and on the downbeat of beat 4. The kick drum on the downbeat of beat 4 is not always needed and it is up to you to decide whether to place that kick drum or not, depending on the song and feel.

Mambo

Figure 3-154

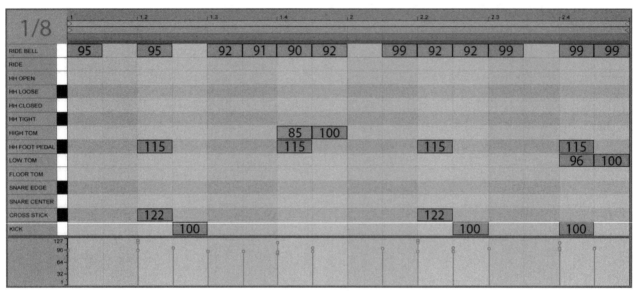

Figure 3-155

BPM: 155

This Afro Cuban groove has a signature bell pattern, which in this example is being played on the bell of the ride cymbal. Even though the groove says to play these hits straight, adding velocity changes throughout the groove will definitely help create a natural feel and sound. Follow the velocities given in Figure 3-155 as a starting point for both the bell and toms. Feel free to change these velocities around to create new color and feel to the groove.

Songo

Figure 3-156

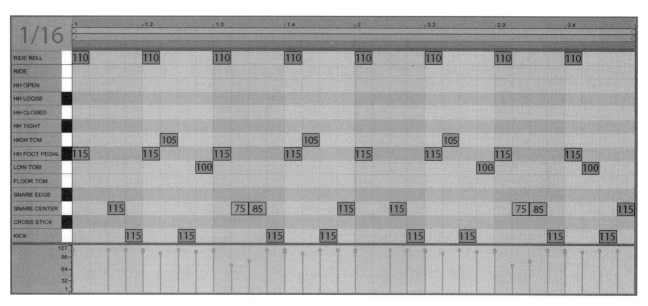

Figure 3-157

BPM: 100

The Songo is different from all the other World Grooves in this book, for the reason that it is the only Afro Cuban groove designed originally for the drum set. All of the World Grooves in this book like the Samba, Merengue, and Cha-Cha for example, are all borrowing percussion parts and applying them to the drum kit, where in this groove, all of the parts being played are complementing what a percussionist would be playing. This groove has a variety of velocity changes due to the amount of ghost notes and tom hits. Try replacing the ghost notes on the snare drum with soft tom hits, or the other way around; you could create some amazing variations!

Mozambique

Figure 3-158

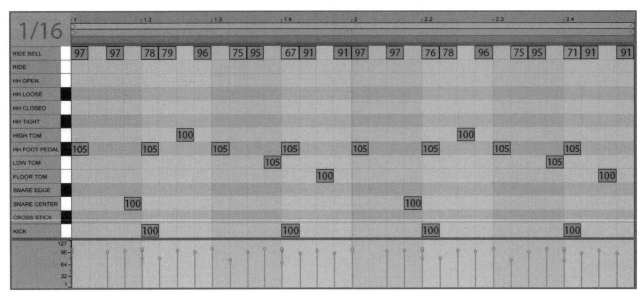

Figure 3-159

BPM: 115

This is an Afro Cuban groove with a signature bell pattern. The bell pattern in this example is being played on the ride cymbal, but could also be played with the sounds of a cowbell, bell ride, or even side sticks to re-create the sound of playing the rim of a timbale. Notice the velocity changes of the cymbal to re-create the accents that would be played on a cowbell for this groove. Variations of this groove could be replacing the rim shot of the snare with a tom hit, to create a melodic phrase along the toms, or to add kick drums on the downbeat of each quarter note for a four-on-the-floor kick drum groove underlying the Mozambique. Try these variations, and some of your own as well!

Salsa

Figure 3-160

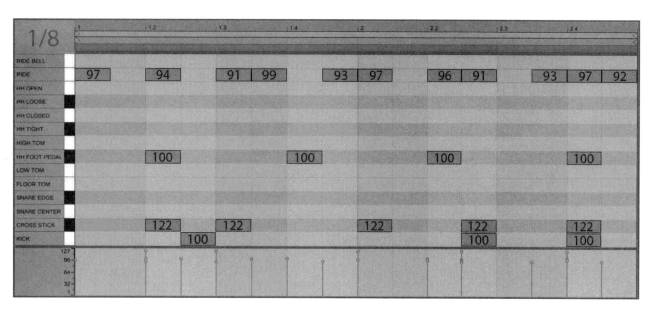

Figure 3-161

BPM: 200

This is the first groove where we mention the clave. In this example, a 2:3 clave pattern is being played with the cross stick of the snare drum, while the ride cymbal is playing a Cascara pattern. The Clave is a very important part of Afro-Cuban music because it is used as a main tool for temporal organization in the music. The music is felt around the Clave, and by using it in this pattern it creates that pulse within the groove. The hi-hat is optional in this groove, but could help drive the groove. The kick drum is also optional on the upbeat of beat 4, but throw it in whenever you like, depending on what feel you want to add. Create your own variations of this groove around both the clave and Cascara pattern, and you could come up with some amazing Hybrid Grooves!

Chapter 4
GROOVE POOL AND HUMAN FEEL

Now that we've covered creating drum grooves of many styles within Ableton Live, we can take it a step further with the Groove Pool feature. This feature will allow us to bring even more groove, swing, and feel to our programmed grooves. The velocity changes that we've covered in the previous chapters of this book are a great tool for transforming a groove that is static and on the grid, to feel a lot more realistic and groove-oriented, but in the end, that groove will still be attached to the grid. For many scenarios that could be great, for example, in a Pop or Dance tune where we want the drums aligned straight with the grid. But for when we want to play a Funk or Jazz tune with more freedom, we want to take these programmed drums slightly off the grid for more of a human feel.

From everything we've covered so far in this book, along with adding Groove Pool settings to your grooves, your programmed drum grooves will sound and feel even more natural than before.

Getting Started with Groove Pool

Let's get started with our first groove in the Groove Pool.

- Open up your Rock Kit and program Eighth-Note Rock #1 into a MIDI clip for this example. Feel free to follow the MIDI Map referring to Figure 4-1 or simply drag the Eighth-Note Rock #1 MIDI clip from the included DVD-ROM's folder titled Groove MIDI Clips into an empty clip slot

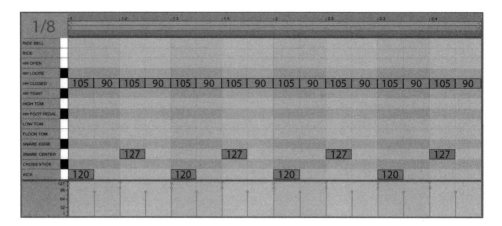

Figure 4-1

NOTE: Title this MIDI clip Eighth-Note Rock. We will be using this clip for further examples.

Tip: To rename a clip, click on a MIDI clip, then right-click and hit Rename or use the hot key (Command + R) on a Mac or (Control + R) on a PC. Type in the new name, and hit the enter key to finalize.

- Launch this clip, and let it play while we go through the next section.

Figure 4-2

Open up Grooves Folder
- Click on Packs under Places in the Live 9 Browser.

Figure 4-3

- Open the Core Library folder. Click on the arrow on the left of the library name to open the drop-down folder

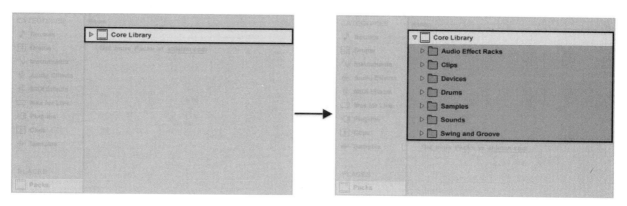

Figure 4-4

NOTE: If you are in need of any Pack updates, simply click on the link in the Packs browser stating, Get More Packs at ableton.com

---

- Now, head into the Swing and Groove folder. This contains all of the Groove Pool grooves included in Ableton Suite 9.

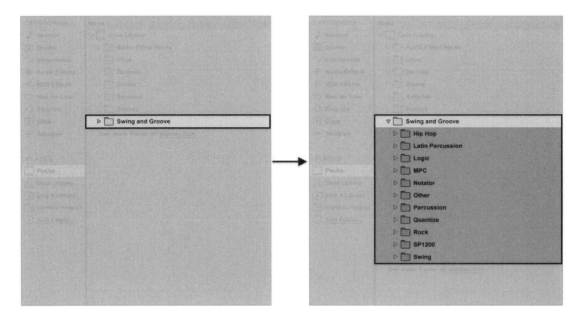

Figure 4-5

- Let's open up the Swing folder by clicking on the arrow to the left of the Swing and Groove folder.

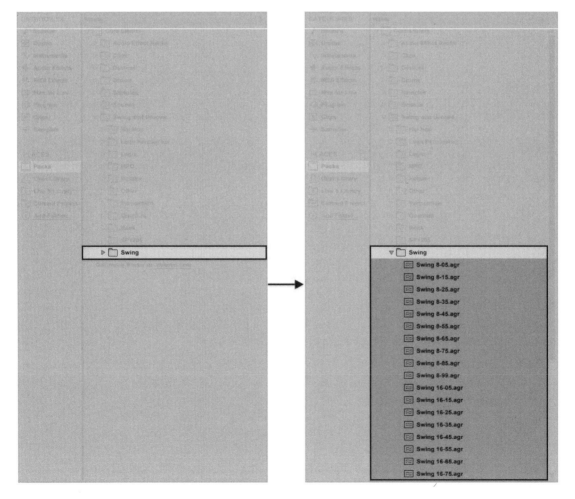

Figure 4-6

- Find Swing 8-55.agr, then click-and-drag this groove onto your MIDI clip containing the Eighth-Note Rock #1 pattern.

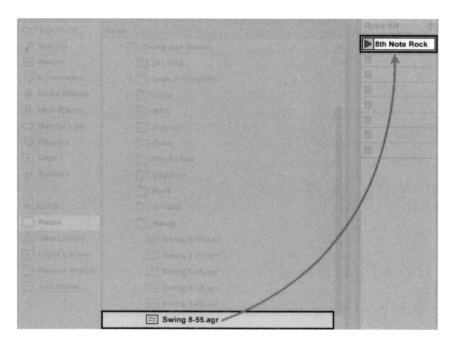

Figure 4-7

Immediately, you hear a difference in the feel of this groove! This groove now has a "swing" feel applied to it.

What is "swing" you ask? For the best understanding, I'll let you hear for yourself! Let's program a groove for an example of what swing is.

Example 1:

- Create two MIDI clips by double clicking on two empty clip slots in your MIDI Track. This could be done in the same track we've been working with, with the previous example.
- Name one clip Straight.
- Name the other clip Swing.

Figure 4-8

In the MIDI clip titled Straight, create this following pattern with eighth-notes on an eighth-note grid (1/8):

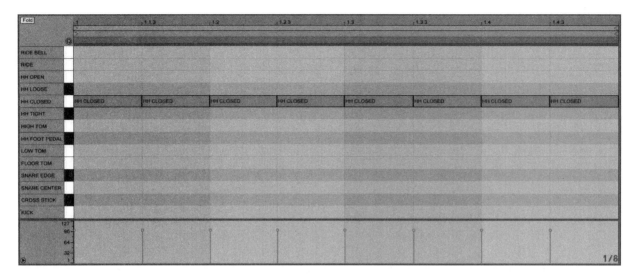

Figure 4-9

In the MIDI clip titled Swing create this following pattern with eighth notes on an eighth-note triplet grid (1/8T):

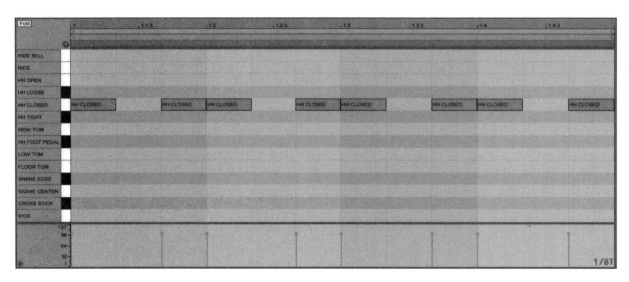

Figure 4-10

Tip: For a quick switch to the triplet grid, use the hot key (Command + 3) on a Mac, or (Control + 3) on a PC, to enable triplet grid.

• Now enable your metronome, so it is highlighted, on the top left of your screen.

Figure 4-11

- Play each clip separately and listen to the difference against the metronome.

Figure 4-12

The Swing clip sounds similar to the hi-hat groove change in the Eighth-Note Rock clip, when we applied the Swing Groove to the clip. Shifting the placement of the second eighth-note hit creates this feel. By pulling back the second eighth note of each beat (to the right), you get more of a swing feel, which has a strong triplet feel.

This is just one example of what is happening when a groove is swung, but what we want to do is have full control of how much this groove is being swung. Basically, we want to have control over how much of the triplet feel is being applied to a straight groove. Although the example based in the Swing clip has the feel of a swing groove, it is still very robotic and computer-based. The true swing feel lies in between these two places of Straight feel and Triplet feel, so let's go back to our Eighth-Note Rock clip and apply these thoughts.

- Double-click on the Eighth-Note Rock clip that we already created to open up the MIDI Note Editor, and launch the MIDI clip.

Notice that the groove sounds swung, with a triplet feel, but the notes in the MIDI Note Editor are still snapped to a straight eighth-note grid. Look in the bottom left corner of Ableton Live under the Clip View Box.

Figure 4-13

You will see the word Groove with a drop-down menu, which holds your Groove Pool settings.

Figure 4-14

Right now it should say Swing 8-55.

- Hit the button that says, Commit.

Figure 4-15

You will see the MIDI Notes in the MIDI Note Editor shift, to fit the shape and feel of the groove setting.

Before Commit:

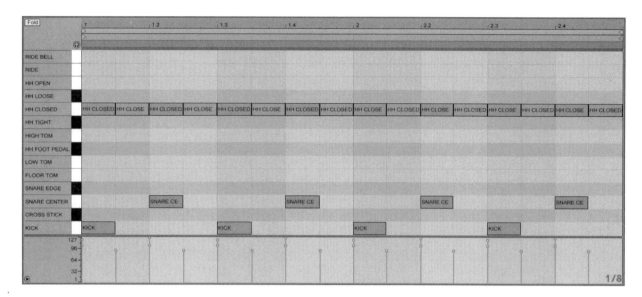

Figure 4-16. Before Commit

After Commit:

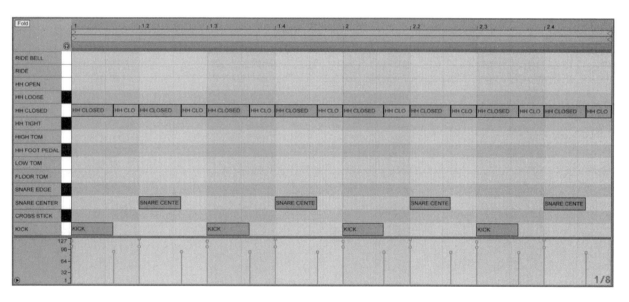

Figure 4-17. After Commit

Notice the Groove Pool drop-down menu now says None because the groove is now embedded into the MIDI clip.

Figure 4-18

Example 2:

Let's try another example.

- Create a new MIDI clip in the same MIDI Track we've been using, and program the pattern Eighth-Note Rock #1 into this new MIDI clip. Rename this MIDI clip Eighth-Note Rock-2.

Let's bring in a new groove to this clip.

- Instead of dragging a Groove Pool setting from the Editor, let's grab another groove setting by clicking on the Hot Swap button next to Groove.

Figure 4-19

Tip: The Hot Swap button is a quick and easy way to search for groove settings. Simply click the Hot Swap button and your browser will automatically open up the Grooves folder in Hot Swap Mode.

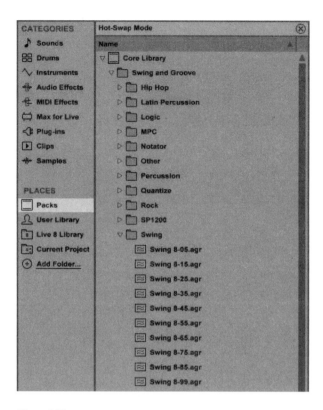

Figure 4-20

Simply double-click on any groove you wish to use, and it will automatically be added to your Groove Pool.

Let's use Swing 8-99.

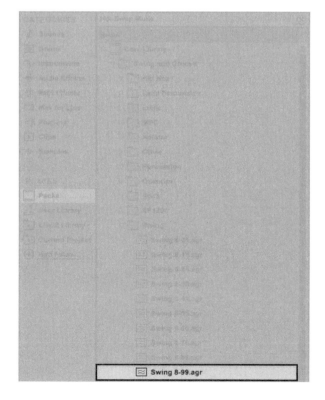

Figure 4-21

This is an eighth-note swing groove, at full level swing feel. Notice a number follows each swing groove: 5, 15, 25, 35, 45, etc. up to 99. This is showing the amount of swing applied to a groove setting, 5 being the lowest amount of swing, and 99 being the strongest amount of swing.

- Now that we've double-clicked on the groove, hit the orange "X" button next to Groove in the Clip View Box, to exit Hot Swap Mode.

Figure 4-22

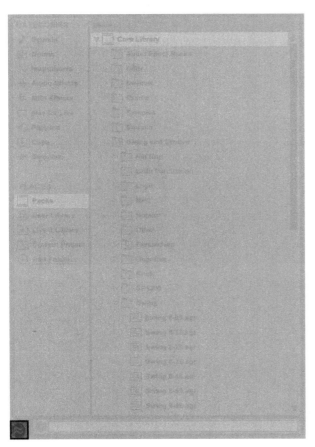

Figure 4-23

Notice how strong this groove is, with a full triplet feel. It might be a little too much for us, so what we want to do is edit the feel of this groove. What we're going to do is head into the Groove Pool by clicking on the Groove Pool icon, on the left side of Ableton Live, under the browser. When clicked on, the Groove Pool will immediately open underneath the browser.

Groove Pool Settings

Okay, now that the Groove Pool is open, we can see all of the previous grooves we have used, along with various parameters to edit the feel of the groove.

Tip: To hear the results of editing parameters in the Groove Pool, make sure the groove setting you are editing is selected in the groove drop-down menu within the desired MIDI clip's Clip Box.

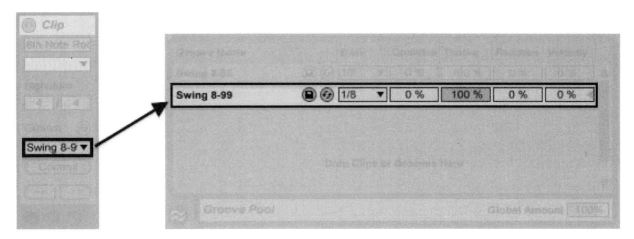

Figure 4-24

Let's head into the Groove Pool and take a look at the groove settings.

The Parameters Available to Edit, Within the Groove Pool.

Figure 4-25

Base

This will determine the timing against which notes in the grooves will be affected, measured by grid value. Right now our groove is based on an eighth-note pulse, so the 1/8 setting will work best in this case. For example, if we are using a sixteenth-note Rock groove, this setting will be best on 1/16.

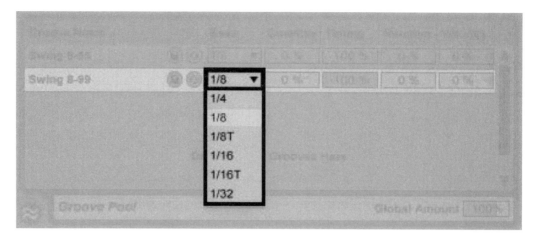

Figure 4-26

Quantize

This will adjust the amount of straight quantization that is applied before the groove is applied. At 100%, the notes in your clip will be snapped to the nearest note values, as selected in the Base Chooser. At 0%, the notes in clips will not be moved from their original positions before the groove is applied.

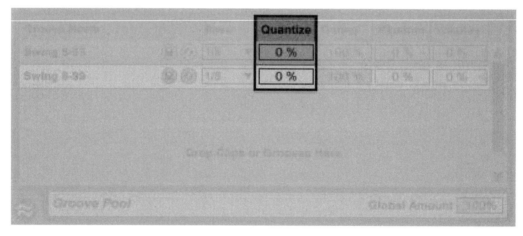

Figure 4-27

Timing

This setting adjusts how much this groove pattern will affect any clips, which are applying this groove. If you see 0%, that means there is no groove, 100% is full groove setting. This option will be very important when finding a comfortable in-between area for a groove.

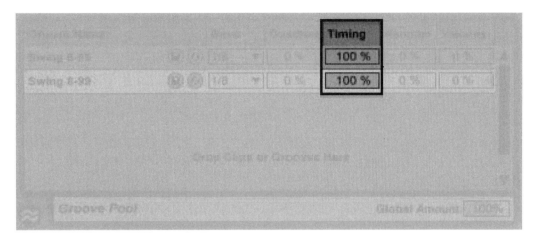

Figure 4-28

Example:

- Launch your Eighth-Note Rock-2 Clip and try moving the timing value from 0% to 100% to hear the transition from a straight eighth-note Rock groove to a swung eighth-note Rock groove. It's amazing to hear the smooth transition of this groove from straight to swung. Use your ears to find a groove setting that works best for you!

> **Tip:** Play with the timing amount by moving slowly through the meter to find a nice groove; simply using your ears, you can have great outcomes! For finding a comfortable place between straight and swing, this setting is where your groove will really bring out the full character and personal choice of the groove's feel.

Random

This adjusts how much random timing fluctuation will be applied to clips using this groove. This could be great for experimenting with new sounds and allowing your computer to have subtle time changes at any given chance.

Figure 4-29

Tip: Adjust the random amount to have slight variations in your groove; this could be a great effect for adding slight variation and realistic feel. Too much could be a bit hectic sometimes, but try it out and see what you like best!

Velocity

This adjusts how much the velocity of the notes within clips will be affected by the velocity information stored in the groove. At negative values, the effect of the groove's velocity will be reversed—loud notes will play quietly, and vice versa.

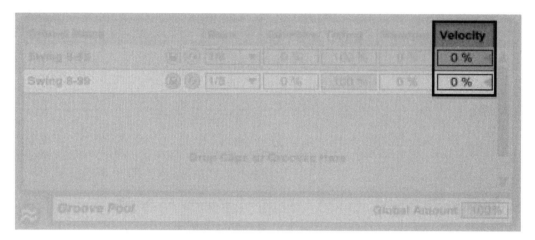

Figure 4-30

Example:
- Let's take a look at a groove with velocity changes. Open up the Hip Hop Grooves folder and bring in the Loosely Flow groove. Click on this groove setting and drag it into the Groove Pool. Now choose Loosely Flow from the groove drop-down menu in your MIDI clip.

Figure 4-31

- Adjust the velocity in the Groove Pool to 100% to see the difference of velocity changes.

Figure 4-32

- It's amazing how much feeling has been added to this once before static groove. Hit the Commit button in your MIDI clip to see the changes!

Figure 4-33

Global Amount

The Global Amount adjusts the overall intensity of timing, random and velocity for all grooves in the Groove Pool. At 100%, the parameters in each groove will be applied at their assigned values. When the Global Groove Amount is set lower than 100%, the parameters will be applied less than their assigned values, and when the Global Groove Amount is higher than 100%, the parameters will be applied beyond their assigned values. This is a great way to equally adjust multiple parameters of all of your grooves in one quick and simple motion.

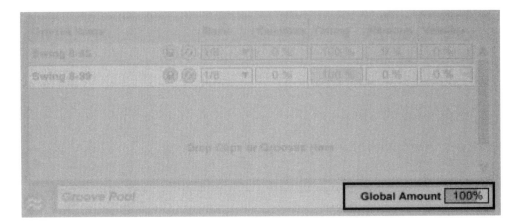

Figure 4-34

How to Create Your Own Custom Groove Pool Setting

Now that you have an understanding of how the Groove Pool works and how to adjust the parameters within the Groove Pool for your own needs, you can now apply further editing to your groove as well by hand. It's great to go into the MIDI Note Editor for any further subtle changes you'd like to make.

For example, let's create a new MIDI Track and add a Funk Kit to that MIDI Track.

- Drag the MIDI clip "Funk #5" from the included DVD-ROM's folder called Groove MIDI Clips into an empty clip slot in the MIDI Track holding the Funk Kit, and throw a Hip Hop 1 Groove on the Funk #5 MIDI clip, from the Hip Hop folder, under the Swing and Groove folder.

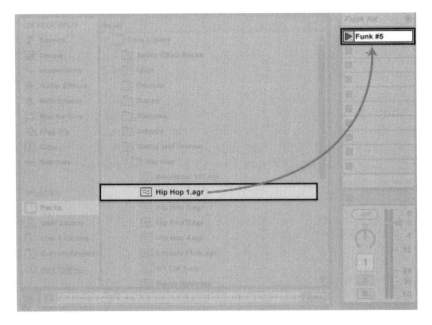

Figure 4-35

- Hit the Commit button for that groove and let's make some more changes to this groove within the MIDI Note Editor.

Figure 4-36

We can see and feel that the groove now has a swing to it, with the Groove Pool setting.

Before Commit:

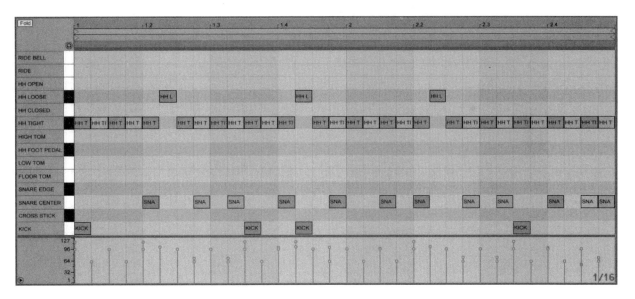

Figure 4-37. Before Commit

After Commit:

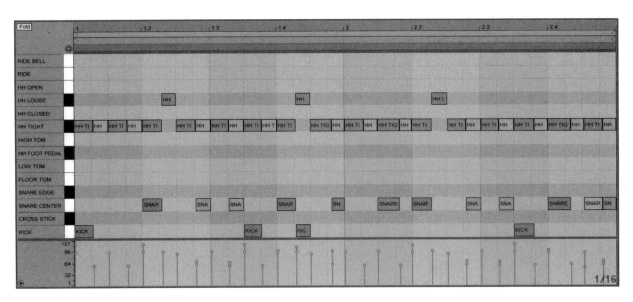

Figure 4-38. After Commit

Let's make some changes within this groove to make it slightly different.

> **Tip:** Zoom in to this groove, by clicking and dragging vertically on the upper border, or beat time ruler, of the Clip View.

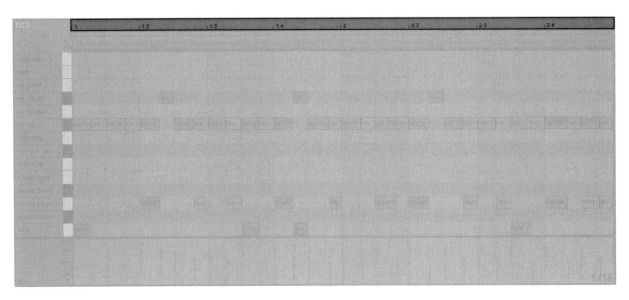

Figure 4-39

- Let's zoom in on beat 2.2 (beat 2 of bar 2); the snare drum and hi-hat are slightly off the beat.

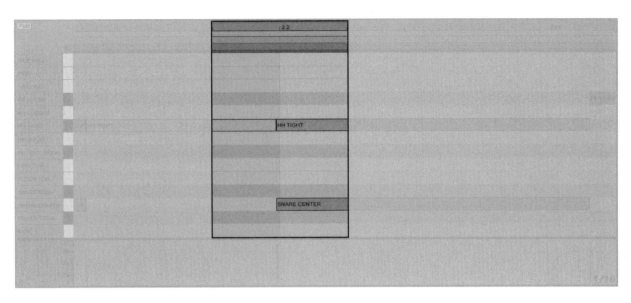

Figure 4-40

- Now, snap those notes back to the grid by clicking and dragging each note and moving it to the grid.

Before:

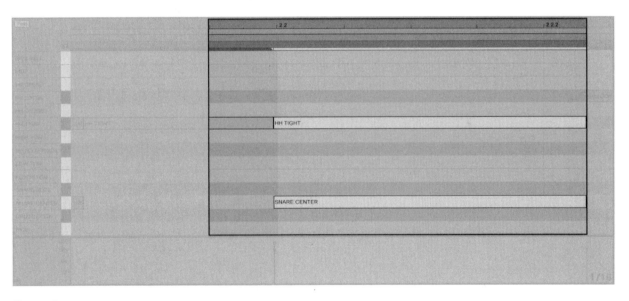

Figure 4-41

After:

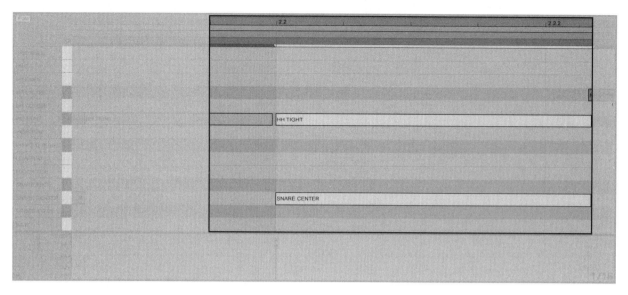

Figure 4-42

Tip: Click on each MIDI Note, while holding the shift key on your keyboard, to highlight multiple MIDI Notes. When adjusting one of the highlighted notes, all other highlighted notes will be adjusted.

Let's do the same with the second-to-last snare drum and hi-hat in this groove.

- Click-and-drag the second to last snare and hi-hat so they snap to the grid of beat 2.4.3.

Before:

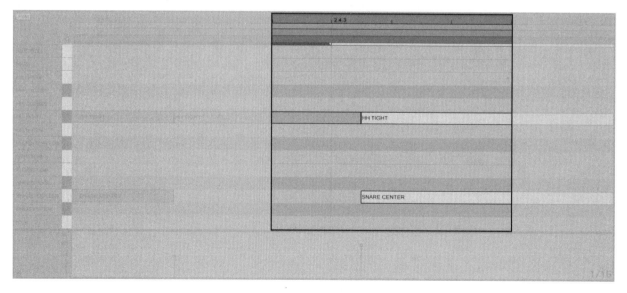

Figure 4-43

After:

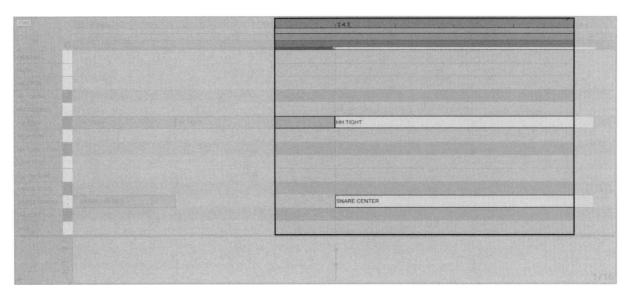

Figure 4-44

These are very subtle changes, but they have changed the groove to feel different in our own personal way. We took many beats off of the grid with the Hip Hop Groove Pool Setting, but have moved some of the beats back onto the grid by hand, for our own personal feel and taste.

Extracting Groove

What we can do now is extract this groove.

- Right-click on the MIDI Note Editor of this groove and click on Extract Groove(s) from the pop up menu.

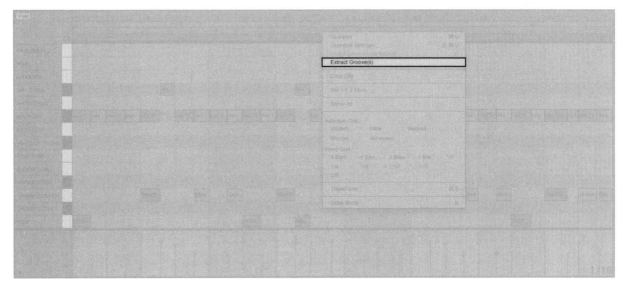

Figure 4-45

- Notice that a Groove Funk#5 has just been added to the Groove Pool.

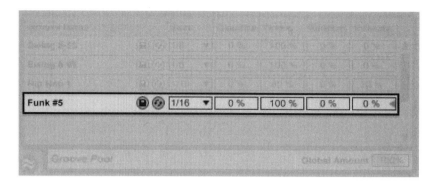

Figure 4-46

- You have just simply created your own custom Groove Pool setting!
- To save this setting, click on the Save button next to the groove name.

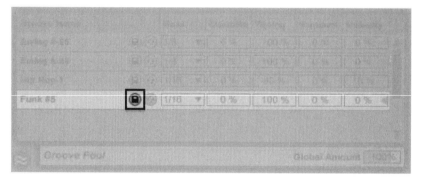

Figure 4-47

You will then see the groove appear in your browser, under your User Library within the Grooves folder.

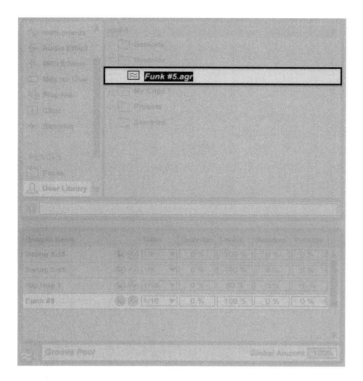

Figure 4-48

- Type to rename your new custom groove and hit the enter key to save the setting.

The groove has now been saved into your User Library under the Grooves folder. You can now drag this groove into any clip to apply your own custom groove to any new programmed drum groove.

Tip: Try out all of the Groove Pool settings to see which work best with your grooves. Some work better than others for specific grooves, but there is no right or wrong way to use these groove settings. Edit the parameters within the Groove Pool, experiment, and have fun with them all! You can save all of your Groove Pool edits, to create your own custom groove libraries with your own feel and sound to distinguish your own drum kit programming from others.

Chapter 5
FINISHING UP

You now have an understanding of drum groove programming of over 80 standard grooves of various styles, mixing Drum Racks in Ableton Live, velocity changes, Ableton Live's Groove Pool, and creating your own custom grooves settings. With this knowledge you are ready to create all of the drum patterns and grooves you can imagine! I really hope this book has helped you with your understanding of drum kit programming, and once again, this book has been created not just to help you learn the various styles of drum kit programming, but to be a stepping stone for your own future creation. Use the tips and tricks within this book to create the drum patterns you've always wanted, whether you are a drummer, a producer, or somebody starting out fresh.

Helpful Tips

Here's a list of some tips to help you get started with your new knowledge for drum programming!

Mix and Match Grooves from Different Chapters
- Take velocity changes, or note placements from Funk grooves, and apply them to Rock grooves. Combine World grooves with Dance grooves, or Jazz grooves with R&B grooves. The combinations are endless and you can create some amazing Hybrid Grooves!
- Try this out: Apply a World groove bell pattern to your Rock, Funk, or Dance grooves.

Boost the Velocity
- All of the velocity settings in this book are a great place to start, but there are no rules saying this is the only way to program velocity changes. Have fun with the velocity changes from 1 all the way to 127. You will never know what it sounds like until you try it out!

Experiment and Try New Things

- All of the grooves in this book are great additions to your groove vocabulary, but there are no rules saying these are the only ways to program drum grooves. Have fun with the placement, velocity, and groove settings. Move notes around to placements you haven't seen or heard anywhere in this book or anywhere else. Who knows? That could be the new sound you've been looking for!

Listen to Various Styles of Music

- A very important and easy way to understand various styles of music, is simply to listen to them. Whether you are a personal fan of Rock, Jazz, Hip-Hop, Funk, or any other styles, try expanding your musical vocabulary by listening to music you are not familiar with; there is a great chance it will open you up to a new understanding and appreciation toward new styles. By hearing new styles of music, and drum grooves played in these styles, it will help you understand the sound, feel, placement, and application of the grooves you've learned in this book, which will greatly benefit your drum groove programming.

APPENDIX:
ABOUT THE DVD-ROM

The included DVD-ROM contains many useful files for your enjoyment. This appendix will walk you through the steps for making the most of them.

1. Begin by inserting the DVD into your computer's DVD-ROM drive. When the DVD icon shows up in your file browser—Finder on Mac, Windows Explorer on PC—double-click on it to see its contents. You should see a single icon named Ableton Grooves Media Content.zip, along with the Read Me file.

2. Click-and-drag the Ableton Grooves Media Content.zip icon to your desktop, and double-click it to reveal the Ableton Grooves Media Content folder. Having a copy on your desktop will allow you quick, easy access to the content, as well as provide you with modifiable versions of the files.

3. When the files are done copying to your desktop—the content is roughly 6 GB in size—navigate to this new copy of Ableton Grooves Media Content on your desktop and open it. You should see the following content inside.

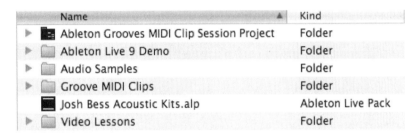

Name	Kind
▶ ▦ Ableton Grooves MIDI Clip Session Project	Folder
▶ ▢ Ableton Live 9 Demo	Folder
▶ ▢ Audio Samples	Folder
▶ ▢ Groove MIDI Clips	Folder
▮ Josh Bess Acoustic Kits.alp	Ableton Live Pack
▶ ▢ Video Lessons	Folder

Figure A-1. Ableton Grooves Media Contents

This folder contains the following:

- Ableton Grooves MIDI Clip Session Project. This folder contains an Ableton Live set, featuring every groove seen in this book, holding an arrangement of MIDI clips within the Session View of Ableton Live. Each MIDI Track contains a Drum Rack referring to each style in this book, such as Velocity Examples, Hi-Hat Examples, Rock, Metal, Dance, Funk, R&B, Jazz, and World grooves. For example, the Rock track contains MIDI clips holding every Rock groove within this book. By navigating vertically from top to bottom, you will start from the first Rock groove to the last. On the right side of the Session View, you will see a tempo referring to each drum groove's MIDI clip, written as a scene name. Simply click on the Scene Launch, which is the orange arrow, and the drum groove's MIDI clip, which is horizontal to this scene will launch.

Figure A-2. Scene Launch

- Ableton Live 9 Demo. This folder contains a free 30-day trial of Ableton Live 9. Within this folder, simply open the Mac or PC folder, which will contain the Ableton Live 9 Demo for your specific operating system. Simply follow Figure A-3 for Mac installation and Figure A-4 for PC installation.

Figure A-3. Mac

Figure A-4. PC

- Audio Samples. This folder contains audio samples for each drum groove and audio example within the book. Within this folder, open the Grooves folder to listen to each drum groove discussed in this book. Specific audio examples discussed in the book are within the Hi-Hat Examples, Jazz Swing Examples, and Velocity Examples folders as well.

- Groove MIDI Clips. This folder contains MIDI clips, holding MIDI data for each drum groove and example discussed in this book. Within this folder, open the Grooves folder to see every groove's MIDI information seen as a MIDI file. The Hi-Hat Examples, and Velocity Examples folders contains MIDI information for the specified examples as well.

    These MIDI files are great, for the reason that you can simply click-and-drag these files into an Ableton Live clip slot, to quickly program a drum groove. This will allow you to import a drum groove, which has been discussed in this book, in one quick and simple motion. Once this MIDI file is within an Ableton Live MIDI clip, you have complete freedom to re-arrange these MIDI Notes and data, using the MIDI Note Editor.

- Josh Bess Acoustic Kits. This Ableton Live Pack contains all of the Ableton Live Drum Racks you will be using to program your drum grooves throughout this book. To install the Ableton Live Pack, simply double-click on Josh Bess Acoustic Kits.alp and the Pack will automatically open up Ableton Live. You will then be asked to install this Ableton Live Pack; click Yes. Once installed, these Drum Racks will be located in the Packs Sections within the Ableton Live 9 Browser. Open the Ableton Live Pack, Josh Bess Acoustic Kits, and follow by opening up the Drums folder. Your new Drum Racks will be within this folder.

These Drum Racks were created by myself, and are now yours to program and write your own acoustic drum grooves. Each Drum Rack contains multiple samples, designed specifically for each style in this book. These styles include Rock, Metal, Dance, Funk, R&B, Jazz, and World. These Drum Racks are filled with high-quality drum samples, which will allow your programmed drums to sound and feel like a real acoustic drum kit, with 127 levels of various velocity changes for each drum pad.

- Video Lessons. This folder will contain video lessons corresponding to each chapter within this book. They are in subfolders divided by chapters. You can simply start at the beginning of chapter 1 and follow along with each exercise given sequentially in the book and video lessons. You can easily complete the entire book's exercises in this linear manner, but for the reason you want to skip ahead to various exercises, these videos are here to allow you that flexibility.

The content within this DVD-ROM is not only designed to add to your understanding of this book, but also contains files and devices that will add to your own future creation of drum programming and music production. The exercises and content within this book and DVD are an important place to start and will always be a great reference and resource. The included Drum Racks and audio samples are yours to take with you and add to your future music production. I hope these contents, drum kits, and samples will help you create and understand the drums you've always imagined playing or programming. Enjoy!

INDEX